Suffolk Dragonflies

Edited by
Nick Mason and Adrian Parr

The Suffolk

Naturalists' Society

c/o Ipswich Museum, High Street
Ipswich Suffolk IP1 3QH
www.sns.org.uk

ISBN 978-0-9508154-7-3

Suffolk Dragonflies
© Text Nick Mason & Adrian Parr, 2016
© The copyright of plates remains with the photographers

Published by
SUFFOLK NATURALISTS' SOCIETY
2016

Compiled by the editors and the rest of The Suffolk Dragonfly Group:

Dorothy Casey and Steve Piotrowski
with
Steve Abbott, Ricky Fairhead, Gi Grieco,
James Robinson, Mick Wright

This book is dedicated to the late Keith Morris
who did so much for our Odonata and was
Suffolk Dragonfly Recorder between 2005 and 2007.

CONTENTS

INTRODUCTION

Some two and a half decades ago, Howard Mendel (Mendel, 1992) published his excellent summary of the state of Suffolk's Odonata at that time, which was based on a period of intensive county-wide surveying. A lot has happened in the British dragonfly world since then, much apparently being driven by climate changes that have set in over the last few decades (e.g. Parr, 2010). These developments led the British Dragonfly Society to organise a period of intensive fieldwork, starting around 2008, that culminated in the publication of a new national dragonfly Atlas (Cham *et al.*, 2014). Suffolk recorders played a major role in this fieldwork, and also continued intensive recording even after the national Atlas was completed. The opportunity has, therefore, arisen to produce a new local Suffolk Atlas, to update the publication of Mendel (1992), and to reveal how ongoing trends in the dragonfly world have affected Suffolk.

The new Atlas has been designed to be self-contained, covering almost all aspects of local dragonfly biology and distribution. Being an Atlas, rather than a field guide or an ecological text, some areas are, however, by necessity covered in rather more detail than others. In particular, emphasis has been placed on how local species distributions have changed since the early 1990s, and what the reasons behind this may be. The reader is referred to Mendel (1992) for a thoughtful and thorough analysis of more historic aspects of dragonfly distributions within the county.

The opening chapter of the Atlas details and describes aquatic habitats within Suffolk, which greatly influence what species might occur within the county, and what their potential distributions might be. Most of Suffolk's dragonflies are in broad terms generalist species, although a few habitat specialists also occur. These, almost by definition, will have a more limited distribution within the county, and populations will be less able to expand even when species are doing well. Finally, the habitat section also covers some of the broader conservation issues that presently affect Suffolk's dragonflies.

The bulk of the Atlas is then devoted to describing the current state-of-play for each of Suffolk's various species. For the present Atlas, the 'modern' period is taken as 2008–2014, and during this time roughly 20,000 records were received by the Suffolk Biological Records Centre (including some originally submitted at the national level). A core of approximately 20 key recorders submitted most of these records, but many more individuals also played their part; recorders are acknowledged at the end of the Atlas. Results are mapped at the tetrad level (2 km x 2 km resolution), which offers the best sensitivity at the level of observer coverage available.

It is hoped that the information presented here will increase our understanding of the County's dragonflies and the various pressures to which they are subjected. This in turn should help conservation of the more endangered species. Anything that helps foster a wider interest in these beautiful insects amongst the general public must also be a good thing.

J. Richardson

Emperor Dragonfly, female feeding on Scorpion Fly *Panorpa* sp.. Dunwich Forest, Suffolk, 6 July 2015.

DRAGONFLY HABITATS

The distribution of a dragonfly species is determined by the availability of suitable habitat to enable it to complete its life cycle and sustain a population. The species and the shape, structure, extent and position of submerged, emergent and floating plants all influence site selection by dragonflies.

Different stages of the life cycle have varying habitat requirements. Vegetation structure and other physical features of the aquatic habitat such as water depth, shading and nutrients determine the success of a site for the development of dragonfly eggs and larvae. As the larvae grow they seek out areas to emerge. Quality of the terrestrial habitat is therefore important for both foraging and protection from predators. Trees and shrubs provide safe areas for roosting and shelter and open grassy areas close to open water are beneficial as they are warmed by the early sun.

Sites managed to maintain a close-knit mosaic of different plant communities will support a wider range of species than sites with a uniform vegetation structure.

Rivers

There are five main river catchments in Suffolk; the Stour, Gipping and Waveney draining into the North Sea and the Little Ouse and Lark flowing into the Great Ouse. There are also a number of smaller rivers, notably the Alde, Deben, Blyth and Hundred rivers that flow into the North Sea.

The source of water supplying each river varies according to the geology of the catchment. The majority of Suffolk catchments are dominated by impermeable boulder clays. Water drains quickly in these areas resulting in a marked difference between average flows in the winter and the summer when the water levels in many rivers are often very low. None of Suffolk's rivers are in a natural state. The widespread removal of riverine and bank features such as marginal shelves, meanders, shoals, riffles, overhanging trees and woody debris to create straightened, deep-sided and uniform channels means that many of Suffolk's rivers are generally unfavourable for dragonflies.

A reduction in water quality in recent decades as a result of pollution has also caused a decline of aquatic life found in Suffolk's rivers. The discharge of sewage and industrial effluents as well as diffuse pollution from agricultural runoff has

River Deben at Ufford.

S. Aylward

caused high levels of nutrients in the watercourses. Organic pollution from agricultural waste such as silage runoff and cow and pig slurry has also had a significant, adverse impact on aquatic ecology.

Water abstraction from both surface and groundwaters, increasing pressure on the public water supply and the shift in agriculture to water-demanding crops such as root vegetables has resulted in a dramatic need for spray irrigation. Rivers such as the Deben with reduced water levels in the summer may suffer from low oxygen levels, higher algal growth and rates of silt deposition and reduced current.

More recently, water quality in rivers has improved in response to the European Union [EU] Water Framework Directive which requires member states to improve ecological condition, particularly by reducing diffuse pollution from agriculture. In recent years, following detailed surveys, the Environment Agency has carried out reinstatement works to improve water quality and riverine habitats. In-channel features such as riffles and the re-introduction of woody debris have enhanced stretches of a number of rivers such as the Little Ouse and the Waveney. The increased range of microhabitats now present in Suffolk's rivers is of benefit to many dragonfly species.

Aquatic plant communities are influenced by many factors such as water chemistry, the stability and composition of river bed substrate, water depth and flow. Many rivers in Suffolk are slow-flowing and nutrient-rich with a mix of substrate - sandy, clay and gravels. Rivers with silty beds are characterised by large rooted plants such as Yellow Water-lily *Nuphar lutea* and pondweeds. Sediments accumulating on the shallow margins are typically colonised by tall emergent plants with Arrowhead *Sagittaria sagittifolia*, Common Club-rush *Schoenoplectus lacustris*, bur-reed species *Sparganium* spp. and Common Reed *Phragmites australis* frequently occurring. Water plants influence the physical environment of the river by reducing the speed of flow and water temperature, increasing the build-up of silt and reducing the availability of light.

Sediments which accumulate under tall emergent plants such as Common Club-rush, Common Reed, Yellow Iris *Iris pseudacorus* and Unbranched Bur-reed *Sparganium emersum* provide microhabitat for dragonflies, for example Scarce Chaser.

Banded Demoiselle, both red-eyed damselfly species, Common Blue and Blue-tailed Damselflies, Brown and Migrant Hawkers, Emperor, Black-tailed Skimmer and Common Darter are species commonly found in sluggish sections of Suffolk rivers. Less frequent species breeding in slow flowing rivers include the Emerald Damselfly, Hairy Dragonfly, all three chasers and Ruddy Darter.

Fens and swamps

Swamps are defined as wetlands inundated with nutrient-rich water and are colonised by tall dense beds of grass-like vegetation, typically Common Reed and Reed Sweet Grass *Glyceria maxima*. In contrast, fens are characterised by peat-forming deposits. Extensive areas of reedswamp are found at Lakenheath Fen (RSPB reserve) and The Hen Reedbeds (Suffolk Wildlife Trust [SWT] reserve). Elsewhere, large reedbeds can be found at Walberswick, Minsmere and the head of the estuaries, for example at Butley Creek.

Fens support more lush vegetation and often a more diverse plant community. In Suffolk, remnants of species-rich fen are found in the Lower Waveney Valley, in the valleys of the Little Ouse and Upper Waveney at Redgrave and Lopham Fen SWT reserve and close to the coast at Sizewell Belts and Darsham Marshes (SWT reserve). Dragonflies often found in fens are Variable and Large Red Damselflies, Norfolk Hawker and Four-spotted Chaser.

Grazing marshes and ditches

S. Aylward

Grazing marsh at Carlton Marshes.

Wet fences (or ditches) within grazing marshes can be considered as linear ponds in various stages of succession. Suffolk is noted for its borrow dykes, which are ditches created by the extraction of clay ('borrowed') to build up flood defences. Borrow dykes are associated with the River Waveney in the Suffolk Broads, for example at Castle Marshes and at Carlton and Oulton Marshes (both SWT reserves) and adjacent to flood defences along the coast. Water quality in these ditches is often very good and the habitat in some places is excellent for dragonflies. Marsh dykes particularly on peaty soils in the Lower Waveney for example at Castle Marshes and on the coastal grazing marshes, such as at Sizewell support a good range of dragonfly species such as Scarce Chaser (Waveney only), Large Red, Azure and Emerald Damselflies, Four-spotted Chaser, Black-tailed Skimmer, Hairy Dragonfly and Norfolk Hawker.

Lakes and ponds

Lakes and ponds take a variety of forms depending on their origin, purpose, permanence, depth and successional stage, and their landscape setting.

All of these factors strongly influence the presence, relative abundance, and fecundity of dragonfly larvae. Most lakes and ponds in Suffolk are eutrophic as a result of human activity. Typically fringed with dense stands of Common Reed and Great Reedmace *Typha latifolia*, open water bodies tend to be base-rich and usually discoloured or turbid with algae, suspended material and organic matter. As a result, oxygen levels in the water are often low. Extensive expanses of water are attractive to Common Blue Damselfly which can be present in large numbers over lakes. Red-eyed

Damselfly can also occur in large numbers on irrigation reservoirs where water lilies are used for basking after emergence.

Open water bodies that dry out each year are not favourable for most dragonflies because larval development is dependent on the aquatic habitat. However, Emerald Damselfly is adapted to survive the

Framlingham Mere.

drying period. Their eggs are protected in emergent plants and hatch in late winter when water levels have risen. Ruddy Darter too will oviposit on mud and grass and hatch in the winter when water levels are higher.

Rural ponds and reservoirs

Originally excavated for marl or to provide watering holes for livestock, Suffolk still retains a high density of ponds particularly in the clay areas in the north-east and central parts of the county. In recent decades, many of Suffolk's ponds have been filled in and restored to farmland. Of the remaining ponds in the countryside, many are polluted with run off from agricultural land. Some are heavily stocked with fish and are of low value for wildlife. Some species of fish predate dragonfly larvae and other species, particularly Carp, can cause the water to become turbid and reduce the microhabitats that are important for larval survival.

The decline of the livestock industry, and the introduction of piped water as a means of watering livestock, have caused the abandonment of many ponds and they are now in an advanced state of neglect. Ponds naturally fill up with silt and leaves and if left unmanaged become shallow and colonised by tall emergent plants in the first instance,

Pond at Sycamore Farm, Witnesham/Culpho, with Broad-leaved Pondweed *Potamogeton natans*.

followed by dense scrub. Small shaded woodland ponds with a dense build up of leaves are less attractive to dragonflies, but where woodland ponds have been restored to let in more light, species like Southern Hawker will thrive.

The best ponds for dragonflies are open with clean water, bordered by shallow edges and colonised with a range of diverse marginal vegetation. Species commonly found in ponds include Emerald, Large Red, Azure, Common Blue and Blue-tailed Damselflies, Four-spotted Chaser and Common Darter.

Of considerable benefit to dragonflies are farm reservoirs that have been constructed in recent years to provide irrigation for water-demanding crops in the drier parts of the county, for example in the Sandlings. Species that particularly benefit from this type of habitat include Common Blue Damselfly and Black-tailed Skimmer.

Urban and other small ponds

N. Mason

Raised pond, Foxburrow Farm, here used for educational purposes.

Many ponds have been created in gardens and can be colonised by a wide range of dragonfly species. If they are sunny with varied margins and a diverse vegetation structure, garden ponds can attract good numbers of species. Azure, Large Red and Blue-tailed Damselflies, Southern Hawker, Emperor Dragonfly, Broad-bodied Chaser and Common Darter can quickly colonise good garden ponds. Early successional ponds with bare open habitat attract Broad-bodied Chaser, Black-tailed Skimmer and Common Darter. Emerald Damselfly prefers ponds with denser aquatic vegetation.

Mineral workings

The loss of natural wetlands in Suffolk has been compensated for in part by an increase in man-made wetlands in the form of flooded gravel pits.

Sand and gravel extraction for the construction industry has created large gravel pits in the major valleys of the Rivers Waveney, Gipping, Stour and Lark. In the north of the county in the Upper Waveney valley, extensive gravel extraction has occurred at Homersfield, Flixton and Weybread. In the Gipping valley a series of pits is situated in Barham, Coddenham and Baylham. Elsewhere in the county, disused gravel workings can be found in the Stour valley. Some flooded gravel pits are used for fishing, thereby increasing the risk of predation and loss of aquatic vegetation. However some dragonfly species such as Red-eyed Damselfly can co-exist where fish are present providing the stocking rate is not too high.

In the early stages of gravel pit restoration, the mobile generalist dragonflies such as Common Blue Damselfly, Common Darter, Emperor and Black-tailed Skimmer are quick to colonise. In general, well established pits are of greatest value for dragonflies. Rich marginal vegetation, sheltered conditions and shallow edges favour many species. Of particular value for dragonflies are the Glemsford pits on the River Stour and the pits in the Lark valley at Lackford, now known as Lackford Lakes (a Suffolk Wildlife Trust reserve).

Lake at West Stow Country Park, a restored gravel pit in the same complex as Lackford Lakes.

The dragonfly list and status in Suffolk

The Suffolk dragonfly fauna currently comprises 35 confirmed species, of which 24 are resident breeders, nine are migrants or vagrants, and two are now locally extinct (both having last been seen during the mid-twentieth century). In addition, one other vagrant may have occurred, but uncertainties exist about identification.

B: Breeds, M: Migrant/Vagrant, E: Locally Extinct.

Willow Emerald Damselfly	*Chalcolestes viridis*	B	recent colonist (2007)
Southern Emerald Damselfly	*Lestes barbarus*	M	one in 2009
Scarce Emerald Damselfly	*Lestes dryas*	B	
Emerald Damselfly	*Lestes sponsa*	B	
Banded Demoiselle	*Calopteryx splendens*	B	
White-legged Damselfly	*Platycnemis pennipes*	B	
Small Red Damselfly	*Ceriagrion tenellum*	E	since 1950s
Azure Damselfly	*Coenagrion puella*	B	
Variable Damselfly	*Coenagrion pulchellum*	B	
Common Blue Damselfly	*Enallagma cyathigerum*	B	
Red-eyed Damselfly	*Erythromma najas*	B	
Small Red-eyed Damselfly	*Erythromma viridulum*	B	recent colonist (2001)
Blue-tailed Damselfly	*Ischnura elegans*	B	
Large Red Damselfly	*Pyrrhosoma nymphula*	B	
Southern Migrant Hawker	*Aeshna affinis*	M	one in 2015
Southern Hawker	*Aeshna cyanea*	B	
Brown Hawker	*Aeshna grandis*	B	
Common Hawker	*Aeshna juncea*	M	few records
Migrant Hawker	*Aeshna mixta*	B	
Norfolk Hawker	*Anaciaeshna isoceles*	B	
Vagrant Emperor	*Anax ephippiger*	M	
Emperor Dragonfly	*Anax imperator*	B	
Lesser Emperor	*Anax parthenope*	M	
Hairy Dragonfly	*Brachytron pratense*	B	
Downy Emerald	*Cordulia aenea*	E	since 1940s
White-faced Darter	*Leucorrhinia dubia*	?	see text
Large White-faced Darter	*Leucorrhinia pectoralis*	M	two in 2012
Broad-bodied Chaser	*Libellula depressa*	B	
Scarce Chaser	*Libellula fulva*	B	
Four-spotted Chaser	*Libellula quadrimaculata*	B	
Black-tailed Skimmer	*Orthetrum cancellatum*	B	
Black Darter	*Sympetrum danae*	M	
Yellow-winged Darter	*Sympetrum flaveolum*	M	
Red-veined Darter	*Sympetrum fonscolombii*	M	has probably bred
Ruddy Darter	*Sympetrum sanguineum*	B	
Common Darter	*Sympetrum striolatum*	B	

N. B. Beautiful Demoiselle *Calopteryx virgo* breeds at a nearby site in Essex and is a possible coloniser in the near future.

GUIDE TO SPECIES SECTIONS AND TO RECORDING

The bulk of the Atlas which follows comprises a detailed analysis of the current state of play for all species of Odonata recorded from the Watsonian vice-counties of East Suffolk (VC25) and West Suffolk (VC26), with a brief mention of species that occur very close to the county boundary, and which might thus be recorded in the short to medium term future. Records of new migrant species of Continental origin might perhaps also be anticipated in the near future, but because of uncertainties as to which species might be involved, these have not been covered. Neither have species once described as having occurred in Suffolk, but where records are now thought to be doubtful. Readers are referred to Mendel (1992) for a discussion of these species.

Each species report follows a common template. First there is a general **introduction**, highlighting key visual and behavioural features. This is not, however, meant to substitute for a field guide. There then follows a brief section describing aspects of **biology**, such as life-cycle duration and phenology. Flight period histograms are shown that plot the number of records in the Suffolk dragonfly database for each species at weekly intervals throughout the year. As well as revealing the main flight period, such diagrams also indirectly serve (by way of the y-axis scaling) as an indication of how common each species is within the country. The next section briefly describes species **habitat** preferences, both in general and in relation to Suffolk. The main part of the species texts then covers **distribution**, both globally, within Britain and, most importantly, within Suffolk. Emphasis is given to how modern distributions have changed since the work of Mendel (1992). Each species description also has a map that shows distributions plotted at a tetrad level. Three time periods are shown: i) prior to 1993 (small blue dots). This is essentially the information available to Mendel (1992), ii) 2008–2014 (large red dots). This is the modern data obtained during recent targeted survey work, iii) 1993–2007 (small yellow dots; overlaying red, but hidden by blue). Data between the time of Mendel's fieldwork and modern surveys is relatively sparse in comparison to that for the two other periods (due to reduced recorder effort and to the accidental loss of some data), and this needs to be borne in mind when interpreting the maps. Such intermediate data is however included to help indicate timings for any ongoing trends. Finally, species descriptions end with a section on **conservation** which highlights any ongoing local issues.

Within the species sections, both long-established English names and Latin names are used, although the European vernacular names favoured by Dijkstra & Lewington (2006) are also quoted. The use of standard reference texts such as Askew, 1988; Boudot & Kalkman, 2015; Brooks & Lewington, 2004; Brooks *et al.*, 2014; Cham *et al.*, 2014; Corbet & Brooks, 2008; Dijkstra & Lewington, 2006; Hammond, 1977 and Mendel, 1992 to source background information should be taken as implicit within the write-ups; more specialist texts are referenced in full. Information on the national conservation status of species is taken from Daguet *et al.*, 2008.

Further background to recording

Records in the Suffolk dragonfly database refer to reports of individual species where sufficiently accurate location and date information exists to create a meaningful and useful entry. A few, mostly older, records can be assigned only to a particular 10 km x 10 km square, and have not been mapped in the present Atlas; most records have been defined to at least tetrad accuracy (2km x 2km), with use of six figure grid references becoming increasingly important in recent years, and modern GPS technology sometimes providing even higher accuracy. During the period 2008–2014 some 20,000 records were received, which compares with roughly 6,500 for the period 1980–1992 analysed by Mendel (1992). In the current Atlas, reports of the various life cycle stages have not been distinguished during mapping, though the proportion of records referring to anything other than flying adults will be tiny (the one exception being the Willow Emerald Damselfly, where the characteristic scars left after egg-laying can be relatively easy to find and identify). Maps similarly do not distinguish between breeding records (either attempted or successful) and records of individuals in non-breeding habitat, and particularly with mobile species such as Common Darter this needs to be borne in mind. With the recent publication of good ID guides for larvae and exuviae (e.g. Cham, 2012; Brochard *et al.*, 2012; Brochard & van der Ploeg, 2014), the proportion of records referring to immature stages will hopefully increase in years to come. The finding of exuviae also provides irrefutable proof of successful breeding at a particular site.

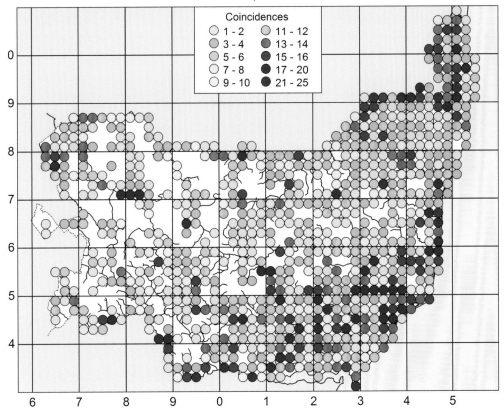

Figure 1: Number of dragonfly species recorded from individual tetrads within the county during the period 2008–2014.

Figure 1 shows the number of dragonfly species recorded in each tetrad within Suffolk during the modern recording period. This map reflects two different factors, namely species diversity and recording effort. Some areas of Suffolk, such as the Waveney valley and Fenland, contain a rich variety of suitable habitats for dragonflies and will thus hold a large number of species. Other areas such as Breckland and some intensively agricultural parts of central and west Suffolk will, by contrast, be intrinsically species-poor. On top of such factors, the effects of recording intensity also come into play. The very high diversity seen in south-east Suffolk thus reflects not only the presence of much suitable habitat, but also the presence of many active recorders in the Ipswich area. Wandering individuals or locally scarce species are thus most readily detected in this region, and a greater proportion of water-bodies will have been visited than elsewhere. This recording bias needs to be remembered when interpreting the maps. Other forms of more specific recording bias also need to be taken into account. Early- and late-flying species (such as Large Red Damselfly and Migrant Hawker, respectively) may thus appear less widespread than is truly the case, simply because not all recorders are active during the species' flight seasons. Species with a very short flight period will also be subject to similar effects.

S. Aylward

Large Red Damselfly, female. 24th May 2015. An early-flying species that may sometimes go under-recorded.

WILLOW EMERALD DAMSELFLY
(Western Willow Spreadwing)

Chalcolestes viridis

Willow Emerald Damselfly, male. Alton Water, Suffolk, 21st September 2012.

T. Caroen

Introduction
Willow Emerald Damselflies are typical of the emeralds with 'spread wings' at rest. It has colonised Britain recently and most notably was first recorded in Suffolk. Unlike Suffolk's other emeralds it does not have blue pruinescence on the thorax or abdomen. The pterostigma is a thin brown rectangle with a pale centre at all ages. They are a vivid green colour with pale appendages. They tend to be found on trees and bushes above the normal level of other damselflies so that a day's recording in July and August now requires you to look up a lot more rather than concentrating on the marginal vegetation. The females oviposit in trees which overhang water and leave a characteristic scar on the bark. Larvae do not hatch until the spring when they fall into the water, the adults emerging in late summer.

Willow Emerald oviposition scars. Alton Water, Suffolk, April 2012.

A. Parr

Biology

On the Continent the larvae grow and develop in the same year. It is not yet known whether this is true in Suffolk though this is almost certainly the case. The adults in Britain typically fly between early July and late October, Suffolk extreme dates being 1st July [2011] and 13th November [2011]. In some cases they can be found in large numbers. Females mainly oviposit in tandem, the eggs being placed into young branches of trees and bushes which overhang water. So far Alder, willows, Ash, Hawthorn, Elder and Bramble have been used in Suffolk. The characteristic tract-like scar pattern can be used to record the species when adults are not to be found. The first north Suffolk record was identified in this way by Andrew Easton.

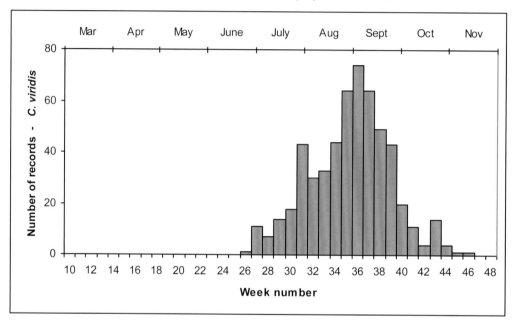

Habitat

Willow Emeralds are found in still and slow-moving water such as ponds, lakes, reservoirs, and rivers which have trees and shrubs in close proximity. It does not inhabit areas that dry out, unlike Suffolk's other emerald damselflies, though it can reportedly do so on the Continent. The adults are generally found on the trees and shrubs in sunlit areas that are sheltered from the wind, though they may sometimes use lower vegetation. In still, fine weather they can be high up at the top of waterside or nearby trees and other vegetation. Looking along the edge of Alders and willows for the adults resting at a 45° angle can be a successful way of finding the species, even at some distance. Otherwise they can be noticed as they fly up to feed on a passing insect. In dull conditions they may retreat into the vegetation, as they may during ovipositing.

Although they may be abundant in good, clean water they can also be found in less favourable locations such as farm run-offs.

Distribution

Willow Emerald Damselflies occur in parts of North Africa and most of Europe up to 53° 30′N; an eastern species, *Lestes parvidens*, occurs from the Balkans eastwards. It has been extending its range and has been known to be present on the Channel Islands since the 1940s. The first accepted record for Britain was a dead specimen near Pevensey, East Sussex, in 1979. An exuvia was next found at Cliffe Marshes in Kent in 1992, without any adults being recorded there. On 17 August 2007 an adult female was then found by Suffolk naturalist Will Brame just south of Loompit Lake in Trimley St Martin; it was photographed the same day. It is suspected that this individual arrived on the same plume of warm air from the near Continent as the insects that carried the Bluetongue virus that

N. Mason

Willow Emerald Damselfly, female. The first modern UK sighting. Trimley, Suffolk, 17th August 2007.

T. Caroen

Willow Emerald Damselfly, pair with female ovipositing. Sudbury Mill, Suffolk, 30th September 2014

arrived in Britain for the first time ever during summer 2007 (Parr, 2009). It is likely that other Willow Emeralds arrived at the same time. There were no records in 2008, probably because the species was overlooked, but in 2009 over 400 individuals were reported in Suffolk. The majority of these were in the south-east of the county. There was also a single sighting at Strumpshaw Fen in Norfolk. At least one of the individuals seen was a teneral and there were many records of females ovipositing. It appears that a population was already established in Suffolk. Large populations in 2009 were found by the River Deben at Loudham, at Staverton Lakes and at Alton Water. Dragonfly Atlas recorders were able to find Willow Emeralds at over 30 separate locations.

The spread of Willow Emerald Damselfly has continued since its establishment in Suffolk, with strong populations now present in many areas of east Norfolk, Essex and north Kent in addition to those in Suffolk, although the county still remains the species' stronghold in Britain. In 2014 there was significant range expansion, with new county records for Cambridgeshire, Hertfordshire and Surrey, and with many new sites discovered in west Suffolk. These included Knettishall Heath, Herringswell, Ickworth Park and Clare Country Park. They were also recorded at Lound Lakes in the very north-east of the county as well as Carlton Marshes and Leathes Ham, Lowestoft. An established population also exists at Corton. As a post-script it should be noted that 2015 also saw further range expansion, and in Suffolk there was an important new record (not mapped) from Lakenheath Fen.

The map suggests that in Suffolk there has been some movement along the freshwater courses of the Deben, Gipping and Stour, though on a national level more random disposal is clearly also possible. Whether or not the colonisation has been climate change induced it seems likely that there will be further range expansion.

Chalcolestes viridis

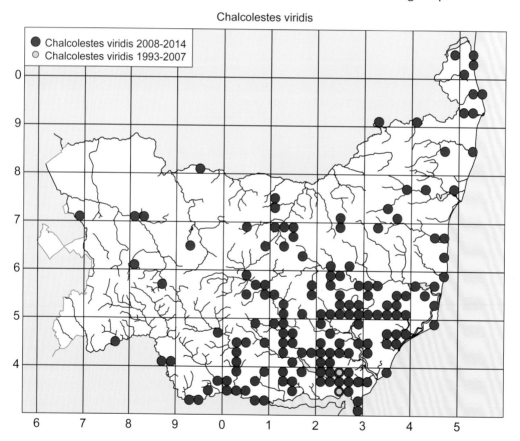

Conservation

The species currently seems to be thriving in Britain, though local populations may fluctuate somewhat (e.g. counts at Alton Water have declined since the immediate post-colonisation period). There are no immediate large-scale conservation issues, though extensive pollarding of water-side trees has the potential to impact local populations, at least in the short term.

SOUTHERN EMERALD DAMSELFLY
(Migrant Spreadwing)

Lestes barbarus

N. Mason

Southern Emerald Damselfly, male. Old Felixstowe, Suffolk, 17th August 2009.

Introduction

Southern Emerald Damselfly is one of the metallic green damselflies. It is paler with yellow on the undersides and on stripes on top of the thorax. The pterostigma is distinctive with the inner half being dark brown and the outer pale white/yellow. The male shows little pruinescence.

Biology

This species has a one-year life cycle, overwintering as an egg. This is because it often frequents water bodies that dry up, especially in the southern areas of its range. It is known to oviposit into dry vegetation, if the site has already dried out. The eggs hatch the next spring and the adults emerge a few weeks later.

In the south of its range it can fly from March until October, but further north the flight period is normally June until August. There is little traditional phenology in Britain to say when it would emerge here, though exuviae were found in Kent during mid June 2015.

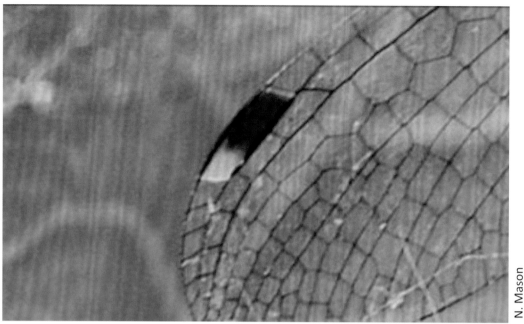

N. Mason

The characteristic bicoloured pterostigma of the mature Southern Emerald Damselfly.

Habitat
Southern Emerald Damselflies are found in shallow, often ephemeral, still waters with emergent and marginal vegetation. As with Scarce Emerald Damselfly this has a benefit in that there can be little predation of eggs or larvae by fish and other animals higher in the food chain, which typically do not thrive in such environments. In Britain it has been mainly found in dune slacks and ditches that can dry out in the late summer. It appears that it can tolerate a little salinity.

Distribution
This emerald damselfly is found across the Palearctic including north Africa (the specific name *barbarus* refers to the Barbary Coast). Its range stretches north from the Mediterranean to the Netherlands and Germany and it is expanding its range. The species first appeared in Britain in 2002, when it was recorded at Winterton Dunes, just north of Great Yarmouth. It has been recorded there in most years since. There is at least one small population in Kent and there have been half a dozen or so other sightings from scattered sites in the country, principally in the far southeast.

On 17th August 2009 a single individual was found in Old Felixstowe. It happened to be in the garden of David Healey, a keen dragonfly enthusiast. Only one was recorded but it is quite possible that others arrived in Suffolk at the same time (as in if you see one rat there are often more around). To date this is the only Suffolk record. As it is prone to wandering (it is sometimes called the Migrant Spreadwing) there is a good chance that others will arrive in Suffolk in the near future.

Conservation
As presently only a vagrant to Suffolk, no immediate conservation issues exist.

SCARCE EMERALD DAMSELFLY
(Robust Spreadwing)

Lestes dryas

B. Buffery

Scarce Emerald Damselfly, male. Redgrave Fen, Suffolk, 19th July 2014.

Introduction
Scarce Emerald Damselflies are one of the metallic, green species that rest at 45° at the edge of water bodies. Males differ from Common Emerald Damselflies in that the blue pruinescence covers sections S9 and S10 and section S1 and only half of section S2 of the abdomen. They are also more robust (thicker abdomen), especially the females. The anal appendages in the male are characteristic and in the female the ovipositor is also longer. Like Common Emerald Damselflies they oviposit into emergent plants where the eggs overwinter, hatching in the spring, the adults emerging in the same year.

Biology
The places they are found usually dry up in the summer. The eggs, which are laid in rushes and sedges, go into diapause, remaining in the vegetation until the following spring when they hatch, the larvae quickly developing and the adults emerging and finishing their life cycle before the water dries out in the summer heat. This ability to remain in a dried out habitat has the added benefit of preventing predation. In Britain the flight season is late May/early June until late August, Suffolk records currently being from 23rd June [2010] to 27th August [2007].

Habitat

Scarce Emerald Damselflies are found in still, shallow waters with plenty of emergent and marginal vegetation. The water frequently dries out in summer. They can survive the dry period as an egg which is laid in emergent upright plants such as reeds, sedges and rushes. Hatching of the egg occurs once water levels have risen once more. In parts of England, especially Essex, Scarce Emerald Damselflies are sometimes found in slightly saline conditions in coastal grazing marshes where Sea Club-rush *Bolboschoenus maritimus* is prominent.

Distribution

Scarce Emerald Damselfly ranges over much of the mid latitudes of the Northern hemisphere, including North America. In Britain and Ireland it is a rather localised species – thinly but fairly widely scattered in central Ireland, but elsewhere very much restricted to southeast England. In the twentieth century it was lost from counties to the west of Suffolk including Lincolnshire, Cambridgeshire and Hertfordshire, but the species shows signs of having recently recovered lost ground.

At the time of the previous Suffolk Atlas (Mendel, 1992), UK populations were found in Norfolk, Essex and North Kent. There is little accepted evidence of it ever having occurred in Suffolk before 2007. Records in the 1950s from the Dedham/ Flatford Mill area are unverified and Common Emerald Damselfly was surprisingly

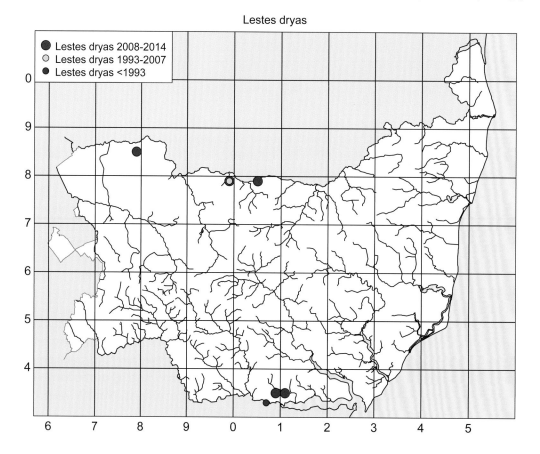

Lestes dryas

Lestes dryas 2008-2014
Lestes dryas 1993-2007
Lestes dryas <1993

unrecorded there during the period. In the 1990s, as now, it was recorded in Essex in coastal grazing marshes and in Norfolk, with relevance to Suffolk, in the Breckland pingos. In 1992, Mendel stated *"it was expected that the Scarce Emerald Damselfly would be re-discovered in Suffolk during the dragonfly survey. This was not the case even though a male was recorded near the Devil's Ditch, at Gasthorpe just 350 metres into Norfolk"*.

The same thoughts were true for the present Atlas, only the outcome was different. The species was discovered in five tetrads, all near the existing populations in Norfolk and Essex. They were first found at Market Weston Fen (SWT reserve) on 27th August 2007 by

Scarce Emerald Damselfly, pair in tandem. Redgrave Fen, Suffolk, 9th August 2015.

B. Buffery

Malcolm Farrow. Populations now exist at Market Weston and at Redgrave in the Valley Fens of north Suffolk. In the south, in late July 2012, about 15 individuals were recorded at a farm in Bentley and three at a farm in East Bergholt by Mark Piotrowski. Bentley is a few kilometres from the Essex border and even further from the nearest population. We wait to see how these populations fare. Finally, in late July 2014, a single male was seen at Brandon Country Park by Adrian Parr. This was presumably a wandering individual. It appears that Scarce Emerald Damselflies do wander quite frequently, presumably because their habitats are often ephemeral, and so it is quite possible that the Suffolk populations will spread, especially into well-vegetated dykes and ponds.

Conservation

The species declined significantly in the UK during the twentieth century (Moore, 1980), and at one stage was feared extinct – though it was almost certainly just overlooked. Factors such as pollution and habitat loss from urbanisation, lowering of the water-table, and natural seral progression (i.e. tree encroachment or build up of detritus) were probably involved in the decline. In the last few decades, there have been encouraging signs of a recovery, though the species remains Near Threatened. The regular cutting of dyke edges would not suit this species.

(COMMON) EMERALD DAMSELFLY

Lestes sponsa

(Common Spreadwing)

S. Plume

Emerald Damselfly, female. Lakenheath Fen, Suffolk, 28th July 2012.

Introduction

Emerald Damselflies are one of the metallic green damselflies that hold their wings open ('spreadwing') when at rest. The blue pruinescence of the male covers the whole of segments 1 and 2 of the abdomen, and also the posterior two sections. The females do not show pruinescence and both sexes can appear copperish when not fully mature. They tend to be found on rushes, sedges and reeds resting at the typical 45° angle. Eggs are inserted into stems of emergent plants and hatch the following spring.

Biology

Eggs are laid into slits made in plant stems, mostly above the water level. They hatch in the spring of the following year, the larvae developing quickly and the adults emerging from mid-June, with insects typically flying through to late September in Britain. In Suffolk, the extreme first/last dates are 24th May [1995] and 7th October [2013]. Within the county, Emerald Damselflies do not appear to be particularly abundant at most locations. It is a species that does not wander and expand its population unlike some other damselflies. Like many Odonata it is more abundant in acidic locations.

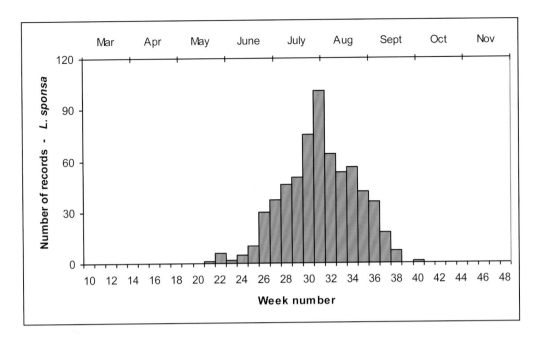

Habitat

In Suffolk, Emerald Damselflies are found in still or very slow-moving waters. This includes dykes in grazing marshes, shallow ponds and lakes and even roadside ditches in the Mildenhall Fen area. The sites are usually well-vegetated rather than open. Damselflies are commonly found resting at a height of about 0.5 metres on sedges and rushes, *Juncus* sp., which tend to be upright. Although they are usually found in places that contain water throughout the year they can survive in ponds that dry out.

Emerald Damselfly, male. Castle Marshes, Suffolk, 30th July 2008.

Distribution

Emerald Damselflies occur over most of Europe, apart from the far south, and their distribution extends eastward to Japan. They are found throughout Britain in suitable habitat. In Suffolk the species is fairly widespread but has not been recorded in every 10 km square. In the previous Atlas, Mendel stated that it was *"common in Fenland dykes of the north-west of the county and grazing marsh dykes in the Waveney Valley"* and added that *"it is surprisingly scarce in south-east Suffolk"*. As can be seen from the map this situation seems to have changed somewhat. In the north-west it is not found in so many tetrads but was recorded in three new ones. It now appears surprisingly absent from much of the north-east corner of the county. The species is not as easy to spot as some damselflies, and this is a possible reason for the lack of records in some areas.

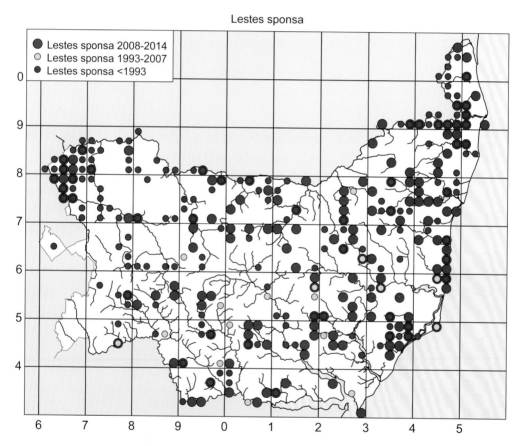

Lestes sponsa

Conservation

The number of suitable locations in Suffolk has probably declined over the past 20 years due to land management and drainage, making it one of the few species to have declined overall between the two Atlases. There is little doubt that the creation or reclamation of shallow ponds, with sedges and rushes, in the county could improve the spread of this species.

BANDED DEMOISELLE   *Calopteryx splendens*

R. Fairhead

Banded Demoiselle, male. Castle Marshes, Suffolk, 10th June 2006.

Introduction
The demoiselles are large damselflies with metallic colouration. The Banded Demoiselle male, when freshly emerged is greenish-blue, but when mature has a metallic blue thorax and abdomen with a wide, blue band across all four wings. The amount of blue can vary. The females are metallic emerald green with no band across the wings. The wings, however, have green veins giving a slight greenish, or in some lights even golden, hue. The female also has a pale, white pseudo-pterostigma. Banded Demoiselles can be confused with Beautiful Demoiselles and Mendel claims that all the old Suffolk records for the latter species are due to misidentification. The wing colouration makes them unlikely to be confused with any other species.

Biology
Banded Demoiselles are found in open, flowing, freshwater rivers and streams, although they do occasionally wander. The males and females are clearly dimorphic, often being mistaken for different species. The wing band width can vary but not very much in Suffolk. The white pseudo-pterostigma of females shows up well. The females tend to be found on vegetation on the bank. They lay eggs into a wide variety of aquatic plants, ovipositing sometimes occurring under water. Surprisingly, for a species that can be abundant, ovipositing does not appear to be seen very often. The larvae normally take two years to mature, being found in the muddy substrate at the bottom of the flowing water. They will bury themselves in this mud if winter flow becomes excessive. Adults typically fly from May until August, but in southern England emergences may begin in late April during warm springs. Current extreme first/last dates for Suffolk are 3rd May [1990] and 19th September [2008].

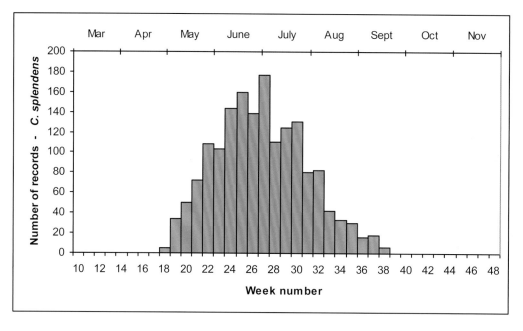

Habitat

This demoiselle is found in slow to medium flowing freshwater rivers and streams, as well as on mill streams and canals. They are found where there is plenty of emergent vegetation in the water and on the bank; but are not often found where there are overhanging trees or other vegetation. They are more likely to found where there is a muddy substrate rather than a gravelly or sandy one.

There is a requirement for vegetation which is sometimes quite lush. Many species of plant are suitable although heavily cut banks where nettles and other terrestrial generalists take over are not preferred. Males tend to alight on vegetation in, or at the edge of, the water, using this either for resting or as a springboard for their frequent territorial skirmishes with other males. Most of Suffolk's rivers show suitable conditions for this species, except where they tend to dry up in hot summer weather.

Distribution

Banded Demoiselles have a range from the British Isles in the west, through most of Europe to the Far East. They can often be quite numerous. In the British Isles they are found throughout Ireland and in lowland Wales and England. The species has recently expanded its range and is now found in the south of Scotland.

This species is one of the easier to find during survey work. The previous Atlas suggested that there had already been a range expansion in Suffolk since the mid-twentieth century, but the extent to which changes in recording intensity confused matters could not be quantified. Expansion does, however, seem to have continued, and Banded Demoiselles are now widespread in Suffolk, as can be seen from the map. They have clearly extended along many of the central, freshwater rivers including the Alde, Deben, Gipping, Upper Waveney, Dove and, in the west, some stretches of the Lark and the River Glem. They are found along the Minsmere New Cut and the Fynn and Mill Rivers, both freshwater tributaries of the Deben Estuary. They can also wander a bit, especially in hot weather or late in the season. This explains, for example, the single record in Hollesley on the edge of heathland.

Calopteryx splendens

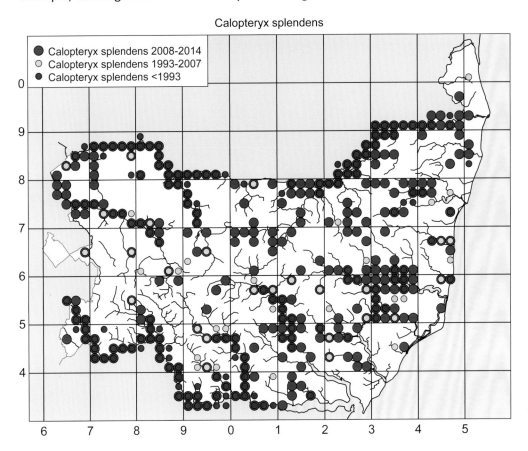

Conservation

In 1992 Mendel suggested that its restricted distribution along some rivers was *"probably due to pollution, however, limited phosphate and nitrate enrichment of rivers produces a lush growth of aquatic vegetation which slows down the flow and produces conditions which particularly suits this species"*. The species is sensitive to pollution. It is quite possible that the general water quality throughout central Suffolk has improved, especially with regards to insecticides, and this may lie behind the modern range expansion. Having said that, there are still several streams and dykes where Banded Demoiselles should be present but where searching has failed to find them. Perhaps excessive flow fluctuations (e.g. drying up in hot summers, or extreme spate conditions in wet winters) might have a role to play here.

BEAUTIFUL DEMOISELLE   *Calopteryx virgo*

T. Caroen

Beautiful Demoiselle, immature male. Roman River, Layer de la Haye, Essex, 27th May 2013.

Introduction
The demoiselles are large damselflies with metallic colouration. The Beautiful Demoiselle male has a metallic/iridescent blue-green thorax and abdomen with dark blue wings. The females are metallic green with light brown/coppery coloured wings and a white pseudo-pterostigma.

Biology
This species is found in mostly fast-flowing freshwater rivers and streams. It differs from the Banded Demoiselle in that it is more tolerant of shade from overhanging trees and other vegetation. It is also most likely to be found where the substrate is gravelly or sandy rather than muddy. The mature adults will move around in the day finding areas where the sunlight can penetrate.

Eggs are laid into vegetation either floating on or under the water's surface. There is a two-year cycle. Adults fly between May and early September.

Habitat
This is a species of fast to medium-flowing, freshwater streams that have a gravelly or sandy bottom. The water tends to be shallow. Often there are trees alongside or overhanging the water. The mature adults are found on this or surface vegetation and seek out sunny spots amongst the shadows. Where both demoiselle species are found, Banded will tend to be in the open and Beautiful in the shaded stretches.

In the east of England they occur in narrow, shallow streams. Sometimes, where the habitat is optimum, this species can be abundant.

Distribution

Basically a European species, Beautiful Demoiselles are not found in southern Spain but are found as far north as Sweden and Finland. In Ireland and Britain they occur more commonly towards the west and the south where waters may be both warm and fast-flowing. Close to Suffolk, there are populations in Berkshire and the Roman River in Essex, and more recently in Northamptonshire. Vagrants have also been noted in north-west Norfolk.

In 2006 a small population was discovered at West Bergholt in a stream that flows into the River Colne and just a few miles from the catchment of the River Stour. This species is thus a potential arrival in Suffolk in the near future.

S. Plume

Demoiselle damselfly (in this case actually a female Banded Demoiselle) showing the prominent ocelli on the head.

WHITE-LEGGED DAMSELFLY
(Blue Featherlegs)

Platycnemis pennipes

N. Mason

White-legged Damselfly, female. Nayland, Suffolk, June 2001.

Introduction

Immatures are milky-white in appearance, and are referred to as form *lactea*. The ground colour darkens with maturity, and fully mature males are light blue in colouration, though of a slightly paler hue than other blue damselflies. Along with its characteristic patterning, including a 'double' thoracic stripe, confusion with other damselflies is thus unlikely. The species also possesses distinctive legs that are pale with a dark longitudinal stripe, somewhat dilated/flattened, and edged by a row of spines (hence the name of featherlegs that is sometimes used on the Continent). Males frequently dangle their legs as a visual signal during courtship.

Biology

Egg laying occurs in tandem, the eggs being laid into floating plants or debris; group oviposition by many pairs in close company is quite frequently encountered. The life-cycle is two years in length (semi-voltine). Adults are most abundant during late spring and mid-summer, with the earliest and latest dates for Suffolk being 21st April [1898] and 1st September [2007].

Habitat

In England, the species is predominantly riverine in nature, favouring unshaded sections of slow to moderately fast-flowing rivers, streams and canals with good marginal vegetation. Particularly in south-eastern areas the species is also found at still water sites such as lakes, flooded gravel pits and fish ponds – habitat types that are more regularly employed on the Continent. In recent years, usage of still water sites has increased dramatically in areas away from the south-east, and perhaps climatic factors are, at least in part, involved in this shift.

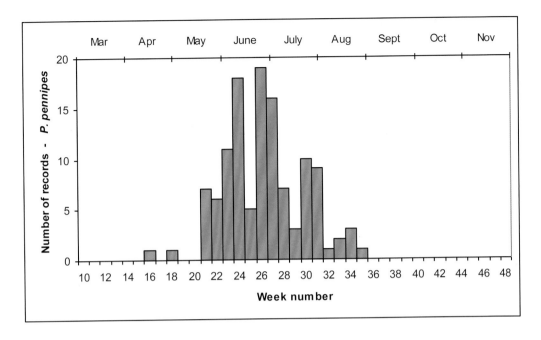

Distribution

White-legged Damselfly occurs in much of Europe except for the far north-western areas (e.g. it is unrecorded from Ireland and only just enters Norway), as well as the far south-west, where it is replaced by related species. Eastwards, it extends into Siberia as far as the Jenisei region. Britain is thus on the edge of the species' range.

Within the UK, the species is known from southern England, the Midlands and eastern Wales. Although records from Suffolk are well-known, there are no records for Norfolk at present. Nationally, the species does however currently seem to be expanding its range.

Mendel (1992) gives a good account of the history of the species in Suffolk. The first records date from the final years of the nineteenth century, from scattered sites along the River Gipping. These colonies seem to then die out, but in the 1940s the species was recorded from the River Stour in the Nayland area. Again records then ceased, and for a while the species was feared extinct. In 1988, individuals were, however, noted from the Stour once more, in the Stratford St. Mary area, and by the end of the first Atlas period White-legged Damselflies were found to be well-established between Stratford St. Mary and Bures. Since that time, the range has continued to expand. Individuals have thus now been found as far upstream on the Stour as Stoke-by-Clare, and importantly, there has been a spread into new habitats, including still water sites, to the north of the Stour. Records have even come from as far north as the Semer area. As yet, the Gipping does not appear to have been recolonised. However, there was a report from 2014 that includes mention of two *pennipes* from near Great Blakenham. None were found when the area was searched in 2015 but the habitat looks good for the species.

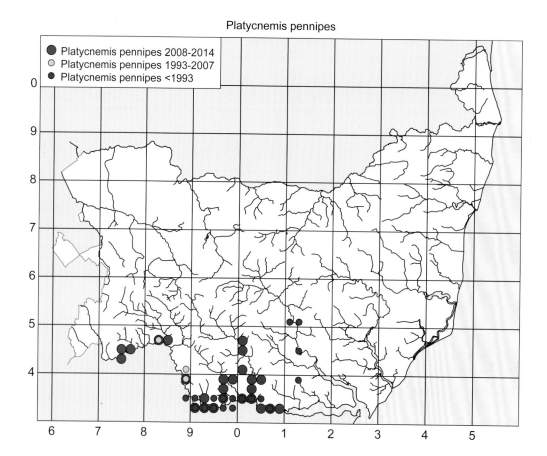

Platycnemis pennipes

- ● Platycnemis pennipes 2008-2014
- ○ Platycnemis pennipes 1993-2007
- ● Platycnemis pennipes <1993

Conservation

Although categorised as of Least Concern in the Odonata Red Data List for Great Britain (Daguet *et al.*, 2008), White-legged Damselfly is of only local distribution and is sensitive to pollution, changes in river structure/quality and to disruption of bank-side vegetation. Sympathetic management regimes are thus to be encouraged. Fortunately the species appears to be benefiting from current climatic trends, and is expanding its range within the county.

SMALL RED DAMSELFLY   *Ceriagrion tenellum*

J. Kennerley

Small Red Damselfly, male. Snowdonia, 27th July 2012.

Introduction
This small damselfly is the only member of its genus in Europe, apart from the closely related Turkish Red Damselfly *C. georgifreyi* that occurs on some Greek islands. Males are rather plain, and have a bright red abdomen, legs and pterostigma. The thorax is a bronze colour with very thin (frequently absent) yellow/red antehumeral stripes. The females vary; one form, *f. melanogastrum*, is predominantly black on the abdomen but other forms are redder. The species is smaller and more delicate than Large Red Damselfly, and the red legs are characteristic.

Biology
Small Red Damselflies usually have a two year life cycle but emergence does not seem to be synchronised. Their flight period is late May/early June to early September. They are prone to predation by other dragonflies, larger predators and spiders around the edge of small pools. The species is a poor flyer and does not readily wander.

Habitat
Small Red Damselflies frequent small pools that may be acidic or calcareous, or slow flowing streams and flushes. They are particularly associated with bog mosses *Sphagnum* species and Marsh St John's Wort *Hypericum elodes*. In Britain, populations are often on heathland, but in Norfolk the population is in an alkaline fen.

Distribution
The species is common across the western Mediterranean fringe and in mainland

Spain, France, Italy and parts of The Netherlands and Germany. In Britain it is principally found in Devon, Cornwall, Dorset, Hampshire (especially the New Forest), Surrey and western areas of Wales; there is a remnant population at Scarning Fen in Norfolk. It has been recorded in Suffolk at Redgrave Fen in 1945 and 1946 and at Fritton Warren in 1949 and 1950 (see Mendel, 1992). The Redgrave population probably died out due to the drying out of the fen and the Fritton one was probably lost to afforestation.

Conservation

There are no populations, at present, to conserve but future immigration is not entirely impossible – more likely from the Continent than Norfolk. Small acid pools in heathland would be a likely habitat for them to breed in.

Ceriagrion tenellum

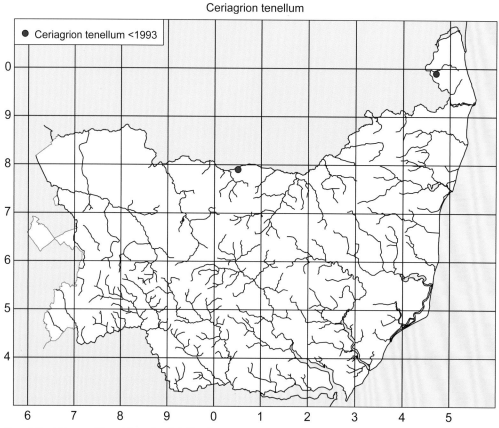

Small Red Damselfly – historic distribution

AZURE DAMSELFLY
Coenagrion puella

(Azure Bluet)

J. Kennerley

Azure Damselfly, male. Woodbridge, Suffolk, 5th June 2010.

Introduction

Azure Damselfly is a familiar species in the county, and one of the easiest to identify, although beginners will sometimes confuse it with Common Blue Damselfly. The males are indeed an azure blue colour, with an isolated black u-shaped mark on the second abdominal segment, and with a bow-tie mark on segment nine. This combination is distinct from any other Suffolk species, although some Variable Damselflies can be frustratingly similar. Azure Damselfly has narrow unbroken blue antehumeral stripes set in a largely black upper thorax. The female is dimorphic. Most are green enabling easy differentiation from the Common Blue Damselfly, but the blue form is rather more difficult to identify.

Biology

Azure Damselfly is seen in Great Britain between April and September. In Suffolk the species is most usually encountered between mid-May and mid-August, though it has been seen as early as 20th April [1933]; the extreme latest date is a little uncertain, due to potential confusion with Common Blue Damselfly, a known late-flyer. The female oviposts in tandem, laying eggs into the underside of leaves and the stems of floating or emergent aquatic vegetation. It is not unusual to see 'hundreds' of ovipositing pairs in Suffolk. The eggs take between two and five weeks to hatch. In Suffolk, larval development takes one year, although in colder climates some can take two years. The larvae feed on invertebrates submerged in aquatic vegetation, including various pond weeds.

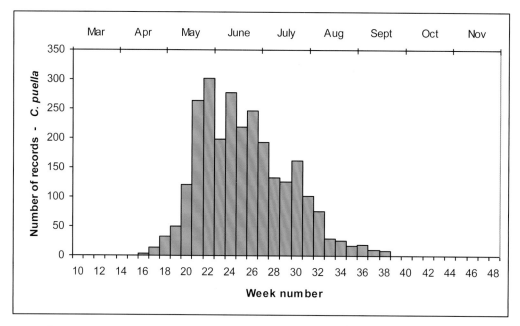

As well as being carnivores themselves, many examples of predation on dragonflies and damselflies are known, and some are mentioned within these pages. Parasitism also occurs, as can be seen here where a male Azure Damselfly has been photographed by Ricky Fairhead with an infestation of red water mites (Hydracarina); these are probably *Arrenurus* sp..

R. Fairhead

Azure Damselfly, male, showing mites beneath the thorax. Carlton Marshes, Suffolk, 25th June 2005.

Habitat

Azure Damselflies are typically found in well vegetated pools, lakes and grazing marshes. In the grazing marshes of East Anglia they seem to favour dykes which are heavily vegetated and have clean water; here they are often found in the company of Variable Damselflies. Unlike Common Blue and Variable Damselflies, this species often visits garden ponds, where a pair in tandem is always a welcome sight. It is a non-territorial species often found in large numbers around their favoured dykes and pools. This species often visits nearby hedgerows and field margins, and can move quite large distances, often aided by the wind. The Azure Damselfly is apparently sensitive to pollution. Excessive nutrient levels in the water, resulting from agricultural fertiliser over-spill, can greatly increase levels of duckweed in the water, to the detriment of this species, and other damselflies. In water bodies where both Azure and Common Blue Damselflies occur it is noticeable that the Azures favour the more sheltered places.

Distribution

Azure Damselfly is a very widespread species across the Palearctic region, its range stretching right across into Asia. In Great Britain it is the most common of its genus, although becoming scarcer in northern Scotland. The Azure Damselfly has probably always been common in the county, Morley (1911) states that *"it used to be very common throughout Suffolk ... it swarms everywhere from Lakenheath and Wortham to Nayland and the coast salt marshes"*. The Suffolk population has possibly increased a little since the last county survey of 1992, although some of this may be down to better coverage, rather than any real increase in distribution.

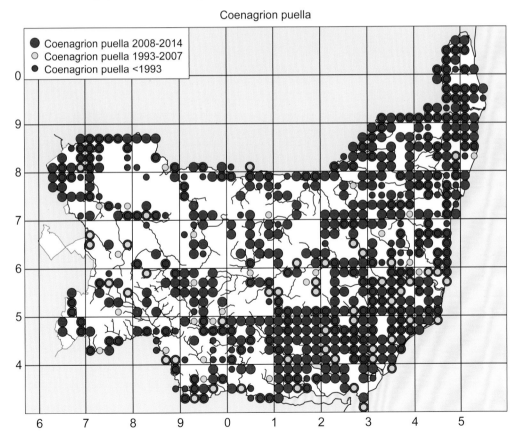

Coenagrion puella

- Coenagrion puella 2008-2014
- Coenagrion puella 1993-2007
- Coenagrion puella <1993

Conservation

Azure Damselfly is a widespread species with no immediate conservation concerns, though as with many pond damselflies it can be prone to local habitat deterioration.

VARIABLE DAMSELFLY
(Variable Bluet)

Coenagrion pulchellum

R. Fairhead

Variable Damselfly, male. Blundeston Prison, Suffolk, 13th June 2008.

Introduction
Variable Damselfly has always been the most difficult of the Suffolk 'blue' damselflies to identify, although with practice identification is usually reasonably straightforward. The male has a dark blue overall colouration. A 'wine glass' mark on the second abdominal segment is a fairly reliable identification feature, although occasionally the stem can be absent, thus resembling Azure Damselfly. If this is the case, it is best to check the blue antehumeral stripes, which are narrow, irregular, and often broken in this species, frequently appearing to form an exclamation mark. The female can be difficult to identify safely, and is prone to be more variable than any other *Coenagrion* species, but checking the pronotum will clarify the species (in Variable it is strongly three-lobed).

Biology
The flight time in the UK is from early April until early September, although in Suffolk mid-May to early August is more usual (current extreme dates being 23rd April [2012] and 21st August [1983]). The female oviposits when in tandem, the female laying eggs

into the underside of leaves and the stems of aquatic vegetation. The eggs take between two and five weeks to hatch. In Suffolk larval development takes one year, although in colder climates some can take two years. The larvae feed on invertebrates amongst aquatic vegetation, including various pond-weeds.

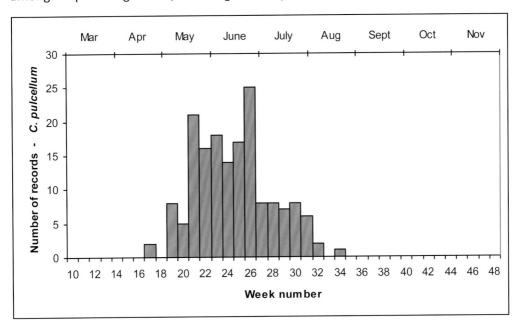

Habitat

Variable Damselfly breeds in dykes and streams in lowland areas. Breeding sites are typically small and generally in unshaded areas. High water quality and dense stands of vegetation are required by this species, with fenland, grazing marshes and water meadows being the traditionally favoured habitat. Mendel (1992) states *"in the north-east, breeding dykes usually have a rich aquatic flora including species such as Water Soldier (*Stratiotes aloides*) and Frogbit (*Hydrocharis morsus-ranae*) both indicative of good water quality. The highest densities of these damselflies are usually found where there is some shelter from the wind that often blows across the marshes. In favoured localities the Variable Damselfly will become the most numerous of the blue damselflies, and species which are* [normally] *common such as Azure Damselfly may be very scarce"*.

Distribution

Variable Damselfly is a widespread species across the Palearctic region, extending eastwards into Siberia, although strangely absent from Iberia. In Great Britain it has a patchy distribution, with highest concentrations in the natural fens. In Suffolk the distribution is equally fragmented, with high populations in some areas and none in others, despite no obvious differences between the sites. The distribution in Suffolk is presently fairly stable, after some contraction during the twentieth century. Indeed, there have even been some recent increases seen, although this may be due to an increase in recording rather than any real change in distribution. Modern sites in the south of the county clearly also refer either to wanderers or very small (possibly transient?) populations.

The traditional strongholds of this species in Suffolk are in the Waveney Valley, with Carlton Marshes and Castle Marshes being excellent sites to find it. The marshes just to the south of Breydon Water also seem particularly very good for the species. There is a healthy population at the RSPB reserve of Lakenheath Fen, not recorded in the previous Atlas. It is conceivable that it was already present at low density in the area but only became more noticeable following major habitat creation as part of the reserve's development in the late 1990s. There is also a good population at Minsmere with individuals sometimes found across the reserve.

Coenagrion pulchellum

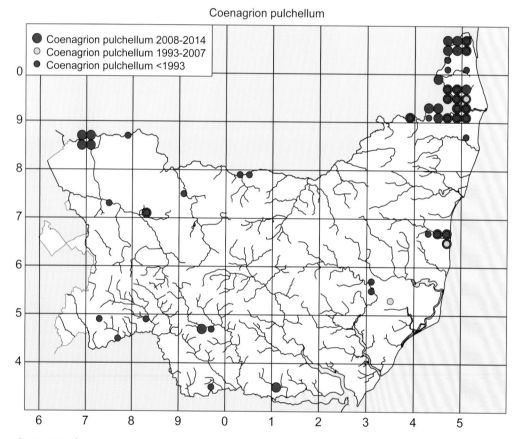

Coenagrion pulchellum 2008-2014
Coenagrion pulchellum 1993-2007
Coenagrion pulchellum <1993

Conservation

Nationally, the Variable Damselfly showed a significant decline during the course of the twentieth century (Cham *et al.*, 2014), and a number of historic sites in Suffolk, and indeed even some of the smaller populations recorded during the survey of Mendel (1992), have now been lost. More recently, fortunes appear to have stabilised. The Variable Damselfly is, however, still vulnerable to pollution as clean water seems particularly important to this species, just as excessive dyke clearance can easily decimate populations. Habitat loss through drying out and lowering of the water table can also be an issue.

COMMON BLUE DAMSELFLY
(Common Bluet)

Enallagma cyathigerum

S. Plume

Common Blue Damselfly, mating pair. Alton Water, Suffolk, 11th August 2012.

Introduction
The male Common Blue Damselfly is the brightest of the three 'blue' Suffolk damselfly species, and also the largest. The easiest identification feature is the black lollipop present on segment 2 of the abdomen and the broad blue antihumeral stripes present on the largely black upper thorax. Segments 8-9 are completely blue apart from 2 small spots on Segment 9. The female Common Blue Damselfly is more difficult to identify, but the species' larger size, broad antehumeral stripes and a triangular dark mark on abdominal S8 should prove distinctive. Females occur in two colour forms, one blue and the other a drab brown, with the latter predominating. When in tandem, the brown variant allows for easy differentiation of distant pairs from the Azure Damselfly.

Biology
Although in Suffolk this species is usually encountered between the middle of May and the end of September, the flight period in the UK can extend from mid-April until late October (at least), and current extreme first/last dates for Suffolk are 23rd April [2012] and 3rd November [2010]. Common Blue Damselflies can be highly dispersive,

with records in grassland habitats many miles from any water bodies. The species will readily colonise newly constructed lakes and ponds, often before any aquatic plants or fish have become established. It seems to need large open patches of water, and when aquatic plants start to take over a site, it can often disappear. At Lackford Lakes it is more commonly found in the shallower ponds. It tends to be absent from grazing marshes where the heavily vegetated dyke systems and lack of any large patches of open water seems detrimental to this species. The female oviposits when in tandem, laying eggs into the underside of leaves and the stems of aquatic vegetation. The eggs take between two and five weeks to hatch. In Suffolk larval development takes one year, although in colder climates some can take two. The larvae feed on invertebrates in aquatic vegetation, including various pond-weeds.

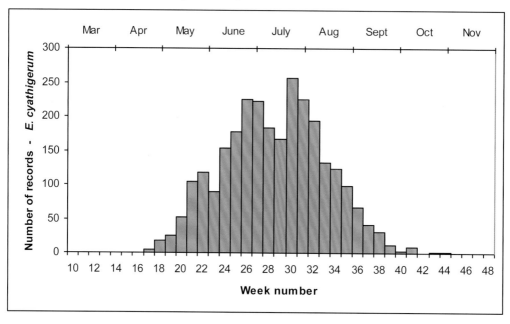

Habitat
Common Blue Damselfly breeds in a wide range of running and still water habitats, and can be especially abundant at lakes and reservoirs. It can often be visible resting on water lily pads, far out from the water's margin. It tolerates a wide range of conditions from acid to alkaline and sheltered to exposed, which is one of the reasons why this is such a widespread and successful species.

Distribution
Common Blue Damselfly is a widespread Palearctic species, occurring from the Arctic Circle down to the Mediterranean, and extending to the pacific coast of Asia. Until recently it was also thought to occur in North America, but studies have shown that this is in fact a separate species *E. annexum*. In Great Britain it is widely distributed, ranging from the Shetland Islands down to southern England, and into Ireland. In Suffolk this species is the most frequently encountered of the 'blue' damselflies.

Mendel (1992) states that *"it is interesting that the Common Blue Damselfly does not always seem to have been as common in Suffolk as it is today. Morley (1911) knew the species at Blakenham, Claydon, and Barnby Broad` and comments that it and the Variable Damselfly were uncommon, whereas the Azure Damselfly `swarms everywhere`. Although he later states that the Common Blue Damselfly was 'by no means rare' with us in June and July (Morley, 1929), such conservative comments would hardly be applied to the species today"*. The Common Blue Damselfly was regularly encountered throughout the county during the current survey, and its distribution has probably changed little since the Mendel 1992 Atlas. As this species seems to be less tied to water than the other Suffolk 'blue' damselfly species, it could potentially occur in any area, although away from water it is more often found in grassland.

Enallagma cyathigerum

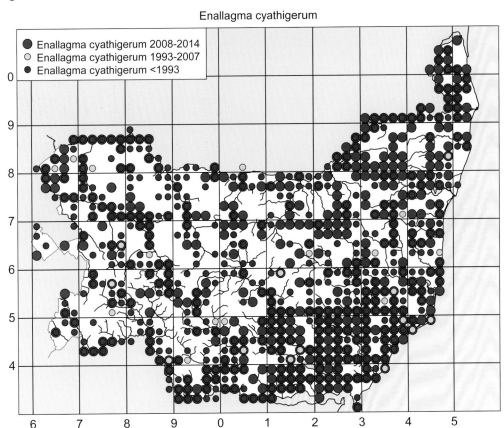

Conservation

This is an abundant species that has benefited from the excavation and subsequent flooding of gravel pits and from construction of new farm reservoirs. There are no major current conservation issues.

RED-EYED DAMSELFLY
(Large Redeye)

Erythromma najas

R. Fairhead

Red-eyed Damselfly, male. Corton, Suffolk, 25th May 2008.

Introduction

This is one of two similar species distinguished by their bright red eyes (males only); the Red-eyed Damselfly is generally larger and more robust than the Small Red-eyed Damselfly, although it is not easy to differentiate them by size alone. On the males the thorax and abdomen are dark greyish-green with blue on the sides of the thorax and on the ninth and tenth segments of the abdomen. The females lack the blue but have short yellow antehumeral stripes. Separating males of the two *Erythromma* species is most easily done by examining the amount of blue at the tail of the abdomen. In the Red-eyed Damselfly it has a vertical cut off between segments S8 and S9; in the Small Red-eyed Damselfly there is an angled cut off along segment S8.

Biology

Egg-laying normally occurs whilst the male and female are in tandem, the females often submerging where they then insert eggs into aquatic plants. Emergent plants rather than bankside vegetation is preferred. Submergence for up to 30 minutes and down to a depth of 0.5 m have been recorded. The larvae occur in 'weedy' areas and develop within one or two years with the flight period typically lasting from May to

August; extreme dates for adults in Suffolk are 29th April [2007] and 20th September [2010]. In spite of being territorial Red-eyed Damselflies can occur in quite high densities.

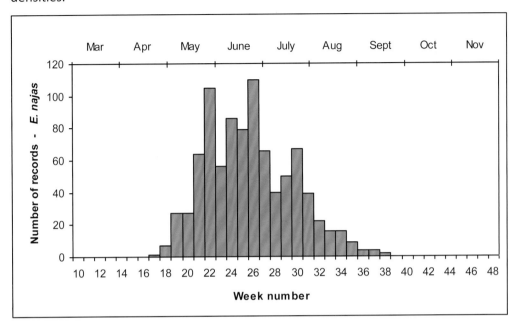

Habitat
The Red-eyed Damselfly has a preference for stiller waters including lakes and larger ponds as well as slow-moving waters. They require floating aquatic vegetation on which they tend to rest away from the water's edge; they are less often found on marginal vegetation. The males defend their territories often returning to the same leaf when the intruder has been dispelled, and they appear to compete with male Common Blue Damselflies as well as their own species. Amphibious Bistort *Polygonum amphibium* appears to be a favoured plant for resting, as do various species of water-lily.

Distribution
Red-eyed Damselfly occurs throughout much of Europe east to Japan, though it is local or absent from the Mediterranean region. It occurs as far north as Finland. In Britain the species is locally common in southern England up to the Welsh borders, though it is absent from the far south-west.

Within Suffolk the species was absent from a lot of the county during the period of the previous Atlas, and indeed only scattered records exist prior to the 1940s. The principal areas where it was found in the Mendel Atlas were along the Stour, with other clusters of records from the north-west and the Waveney valley area around Fritton, with only a couple of areas further down the coast. The species has now greatly increased in Suffolk; it has expanded along tributaries of the Stour, there has been a large increase in north-east Suffolk and along the Waveney valley, and in the north-west there has also been an increase along the Little Ouse and down the River Lark. The species has also expanded into the peninsulas of south-east Suffolk and there are further records along the east coast, while in central Suffolk, from where it was previously largely absent, there is now a good scatter of records with a cluster along the upper reaches of the River Gipping.

In 1992 Mendel suggested that there was evidence that the species was increasing and with many new reservoirs and fishing lakes would become more widespread. This has definitely been shown to be the case.

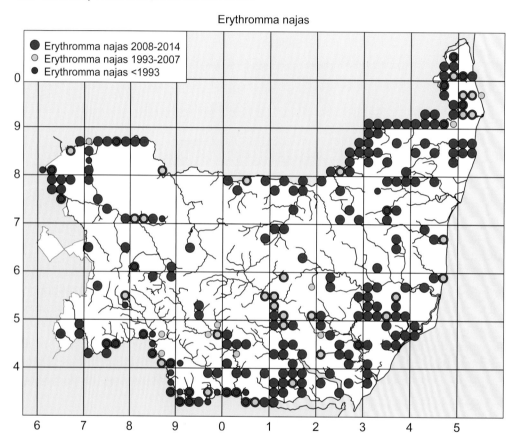

Erythromma najas

Erythromma najas 2008-2014
Erythromma najas 1993-2007
Erythromma najas <1993

Conservation

Red-eyed Damselfly is fairly widespread in Suffolk and appears to be expanding its range. There are no immediate large-scale conservation concerns, though at a local level over-zealous clearance of floating vegetation from waterbodies can be detrimental to the species.

SMALL RED-EYED DAMSELFLY
(Small Redeye)

Erythromma viridulum

R. Fairhead

Small Red-eyed Damselfly, male. Lound, Suffolk, 25th July 2009.

Introduction
This is the other UK species with recognisable bright red eyes, and is similar to Red-eyed Damselfly but is slightly more slender and smaller in size. The thorax in both male and female is a bronze black colour, the female having thin green or blue antehumeral lines. The abdomen is dark with sections 9 and 10 being blue in the males. The tenth segment is not completely blue, but instead has a black 'x-shaped' mark on the upper surface which is a distinguishing characteristic. The blue extends on to the side of section 8 so there is not the clean cylindrical appearance as shown by Red-eyed Damselfly. The female can be separated from Red-eyed Damselfly by the complete, or nearly complete, ante-humeral stripes and the abdomen appears glossy rather than a matt black. Small Red-eyed Damselfly females also often show extensive blue on the side of the thorax.

Biology
The males remain attached to the female during egg-laying and the eggs are laid on the stems of aquatic plants growing near the water surface. The larvae usually hatch within a few days and like dense aquatic plants, particularly Hornworts *Ceratophyllum* spp. and Water Milfoils *Myriophyllum* spp., where they feed and hide. The adult flight

period is typically from July (rarely June) through to mid-September; current extreme first/last dates for Suffolk are 11th June [2006] and 2nd October [2010]. In cooler years this species sometimes seemingly fails to emerge or does so extremely late and in very small numbers, suggesting that its larval development is dependent on higher water temperatures than most other Suffolk species.

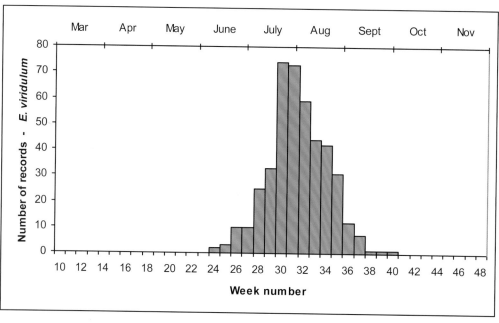

Habitat

The species requires a similar habitat to the Red-eyed Damselfly and is often found alongside it since the flight periods overlap. It is found in still water habitats such as lakes, ponds, gravel pits, canals and ditches but has a preference for smaller (or sheltered?) bodies of water although it will colonise new farm reservoirs. The preferred habitat contains lots of aquatic and floating vegetation such as pondweed and mats of floating algae. The males also sit on emergent vegetation to defend territories and have a characteristic habit of curving up the tip of the abdomen while at rest.

Distribution

This is a southern European species that from the 1980s spread north into Germany and The Netherlands, presumably due to climate warming. Small Red-eyed Damselfly first occurred in the UK in Essex in 1999 and has spread mainly throughout East Anglia and the south-east, moving as far west as Devon and north through the Midlands to Yorkshire.

In Suffolk the species was first found in 2001. Several adults were seen by Neil Sherman (Sherman, 2002) at Ipswich Golf Club, Purdis Heath, including a number of pairs in tandem with egg-laying noted. The species was also noted at Thorpeness and Sizewell at the same time. This influx, which also saw records from Norfolk, Essex,

Kent and Bedfordshire, was the start of colonisation within the county. Since then the Small Red-eyed Damselfly has continued to expand, sometimes being the commonest species of damselfly on some ponds. As can be seen from the Atlas map the species has been found most often in vice-county 25 (East Suffolk) although it is scattered throughout. It is numerous along the Deben and Gipping valleys. In the west it is more thinly scattered, where good sites are quite scattered in general, but in time it is likely to become established in all areas of suitable habitat.

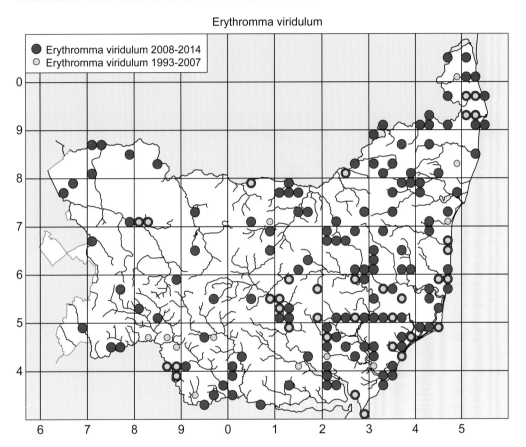

Erythromma viridulum

- ● Erythromma viridulum 2008-2014
- ○ Erythromma viridulum 1993-2007

Conservation

Given how well this recent coloniser has spread, there are no large-scale conservation concerns regarding Small Red-eyed Damselfly. Some moderate degree of nutrient enrichment (eutrophication) of waterbodies may assist the damselflies, through encouraging growth of the rich submerged aquatic vegetation that the species favours; they cannot, however, tolerate strongly polluted sites.

BLUE-TAILED DAMSELFLY   *Ischnura elegans*
(Common Bluetail)

N. Mason

Blue-tailed Damselfly, mating pair. Boyton, Suffolk, 2005

Introduction

The Blue-tailed Damselfly is a very common widespread species. Males, which have a bright blue abdominal segment 8 and a blue or green thorax, should be easily identifiable, though confusion with red-eyed damselfly species (*Erythromma* spp.), or with mature pruinescent emerald damselflies (*Lestes* spp.) may be possible. Females exist in a range of genetically-determined colour types. One type resembles the male when mature (this pattern being referred to as f. *typica*, or 'andromorph'), but has a lilac thorax when immature (f. *violacea*). Another type similarly has a lilac thorax when immature, but matures into a form (f. *infuscans*) with olive-green thorax and a brown spot on abdominal segment S8. Finally there is yet another type that has a salmon pink thorax with no dark humeral stripe when immature (f. *rufescens*), changing to a pale brown thorax and brown abdominal tail spot when mature (f. *infuscans-obseleta*).

Biology

The Blue-tailed Damselfly lays its eggs into aquatic vegetation, often submerging to do so. The larvae normally take one year to develop in southern England, though at higher latitudes development may take two years. By contrast, in southern Europe the species may be multivoltine, with more than one generation in a year. It has been

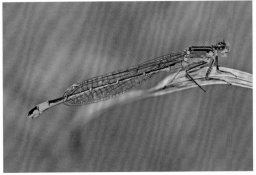

Blue-tailed Damselfly, immature female f. *violacea*. Hen Reedbeds, Suffolk, 10th July 2009.

Blue-tailed Damselfly, immature female f. *rufescens*. Sheppey, Kent, 24th June 2011.

suggested that climate change may also ultimately lead to the development of such a rapid life-cycle in Britain, and perhaps the occasional very late season record now seen in the UK results from this. In Suffolk, the flight period normally lasts from early May to early September, with all-time first/last dates of 27th April [2007] and 27th September [1987]. The species emerges in a "flush" and many hundred can sometimes be seen together when this occurs.

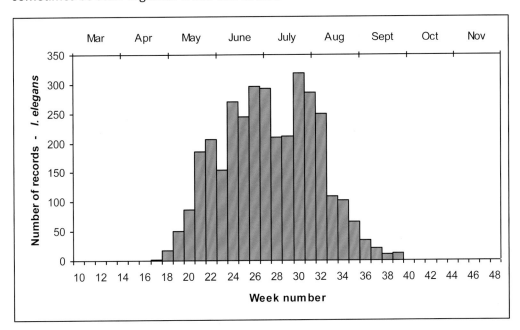

Habitat

The species occurs in a wide variety of still and slow-lowing waters, including lakes, ponds (even those in gardens), canals and ditches. There may be extensive submerged and emergent vegetation present, but the species is also able to tolerate a degree of eutrophication, pollution or salinity (Brooks & Lewington, 2004), when vegetation is often then reduced. Unlike many other damselflies this species spends more time in waterside vegetation than over the water itself.

Distribution

The species occurs across virtually all of Europe, and east as far as Japan. It is however, absent from the far north and is also very local in the far south-west, where it is largely replaced by the very similar Iberian Bluetail *I. graellsii*. In Britain its distribution is similarly widespread, with records from nearly all areas apart from those at high elevation. Within Suffolk, records tend to be less abundant in the west, possibly due to a lower density of suitable sites, although observer coverage effects may also exist. There is no evidence for any major recent change in distribution within the county, although it is possible that some small populations may have been lost since the time of Mendel (1992).

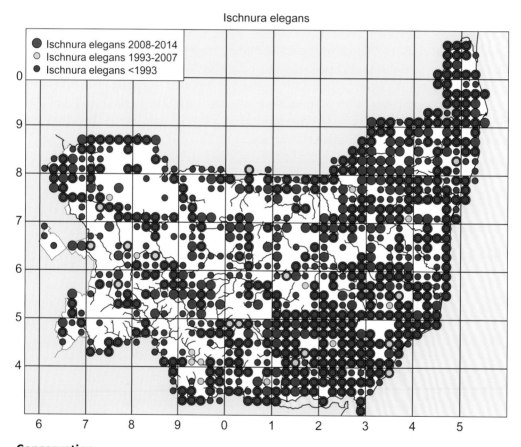

Ischnura elegans

Conservation

Blue-tailed Damselfly is a widespread and common species, which is less susceptible to pollution than many other dragonflies. There are thus no major immediate conservation issues. Although populations fluctuate from year to year, there is, however, some evidence for a small national decline in recent years (Cham *et al.*, 2014). Local data are broadly in line with this. It is also worth noting that while sightings of Blue-tailed Damselfly accounted for some 18.6% of all records during the survey of Mendel (1992), this proportion had fallen to only 9.5% during the 2008–2014 survey.

LARGE RED DAMSELFLY   *Pyrrhosoma nymphula*

R. Fairhead

Large Red Damselfly, male (on Water Violet *Hottonia palustris*). Bradwell, Norfolk, 6th May 2011.

Introduction

This is a medium-sized damselfly that is predominantly red in both sexes. It is a common, widespread, habitat generalist; the only possible confusion species – the Small Red Damselfly *Ceriagrion tenellum* – is a nationally-uncommon habitat specialist that has not been noted in Suffolk for over 50 years. Female Large Red Damselflies exist in three colour forms, differing in the amount of black on the abdomen.

Biology

The life history is described in detail by Gardner & MacNeill (1950). Females oviposit in tandem, inserting their eggs into floating vegetation or mud. Larval development may take only one year, but is more normally of two years duration. The Large Red Damselfly is typically the first species of Odonata to emerge in the spring. In Suffolk, it may be noted from early April in advanced seasons, and there is also a record for 29th March [2014], though this individual emerged from a garden water butt, which was probably above ambient temperature for significant periods during the preceding months due to solar heating. In most years the species is almost over by early July, though occasional individuals have been reported on much later dates, perhaps relating to differing larval growth strategies. The latest date on record is 29th September [1989] (Mendel, 1992).

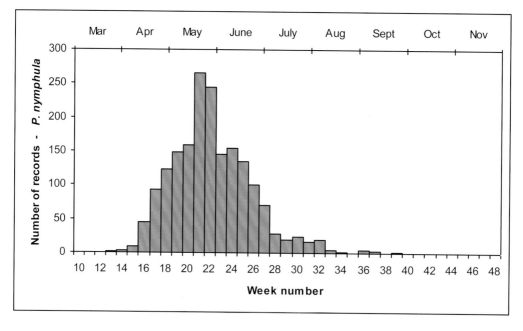

Habitat

Large Red Damselfly occupies a wide range of waters, particularly favouring sites with well-vegetated standing or very slow-flowing water. In Suffolk, records are most numerous from the grazing marshes and wet meadows of river valleys, from fenland and from the marshes of the coastal strip. It is also a common garden pond species.

Distribution

The species occurs throughout most of Europe, though it is replaced in the far south-east by the closely similar Greek Red Damsel (*P. elisabethae*). In Britain, Large Red Damselfly is very widely distributed, occurring as far north as the Orkney Islands, with a few recent records also from the Shetlands. It is rare only in limestone areas, where standing water is uncommon. Within Suffolk, the species is again widely distributed – being found in most areas, though it is rather patchy in the highly agricultural parts of central and western Suffolk, where suitable breeding habitat is less abundant. Population sizes vary significantly between sites, and to a lesser degree between years. Some sites may hold large numbers; Mendel (1992) mentions

M. Holland

Large Red Damselfly, pair in tandem. Minsmere, Suffolk, 22nd May 2007.

1000+ along Minsmere New Cut in May 1991, though in recent years this count would be unusual. By contrast, there are other sites that look very suitable for the species, but where records are almost lacking. It is, however, possible that the species' early flight season leads to a degree of under-recording. This was shown in the present Atlas. Nick Mason surveyed tetrads, beyond Mildenhall, in the far north-west of the county in 2011, a very warm spring. They were present in his first visit in early May but when he returned later he could not find Large Red Damselflies in any of the tetrads. Presuming that this was due to them having finished early that year, he returned in 2015 to survey those areas where he had not found them and recorded them in four more tetrads.

Pyrrhosoma nymphula

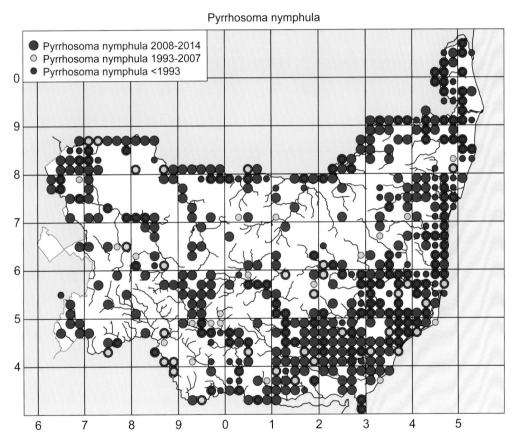

● Pyrrhosoma nymphula 2008-2014
○ Pyrrhosoma nymphula 1993-2007
● Pyrrhosoma nymphula <1993

Conservation

Large Red Damselfly is rated as of Least Concern in the Odonata Red Data List for Great Britain (Daguet *et al.*, 2008), and there are no particular conservation issues within the county. At a local level, the species is however sensitive to pollution and habitat loss. Mendel (1992) suggested that there may have been a decline in Suffolk during the twentieth century, and while its recorded range may have expanded in recent years, probably due to increased recorder effort, numbers certainly do not seem to have increased in parallel.

SOUTHERN MIGRANT HAWKER   *Aeshna affinis*
(Blue-eyed Hawker)

T. Caroen

Southern Migrant Hawker, male. Wat Tyler Country Park, Essex, 1st August 2015.

Introduction

Southern Migrant Hawker shows many similarities to Migrant Hawker, both structurally and in terms of biology. Like the latter species, it shows pronounced migratory tendencies. Males are more extensively blue than Migrant Hawker, and have very strongly blue eyes. Females are less boldly marked than female Migrant Hawkers, and have a prominent yellow triangle at the base of the abdomen. The best way to distinguish either sex of Southern Migrant Hawker is by their uniform yellow, green or blue sides to the thorax. Migrant Hawkers instead show two pale diagonal bands on a dark background.

Biology

The species is one of the few Hawkers to oviposit while still in tandem. Eggs are laid into damp mud. The length of the life-cycle in Britain is unclear; there is circumstantial evidence that it can be two years, but a one year life-cycle would be more normal for the types of transitory habitat that the species often favours. Southern Migrant Hawker is a strong migrant, but this behaviour appears to be facultative rather than obligate.

Habitat

The species favours standing waterbodies that largely dry out in high summer. Such sites are frequently densely vegetated, with reeds or rushes being the dominant vegetation. The British breeding sites are largely ponds, ditches and dykes in coastal marshes around the greater Thames Estuary.

Distribution

Southern Migrant Hawkers occur regularly in southern and south-central Europe, east to Mongolia. There are also a few isolated outposts in North Africa. During hot summers, migrant individuals may penetrate further north in Europe, with recent records as far north as Lithuania. In Britain, the species was a very scarce migrant up until 2006, when several individuals were then seen. Further influxes took place, and a resident breeding population has been present in the greater Thames Estuary area (south Essex and north Kent) since 2010 (Cham *et al.*, 2014). In Suffolk the species was unknown at the time of Mendel (1992), but on 29th August 2015 a male was seen by Brian Buffery at East Lane, Bawdsey. Since the species is one of a group responding positively to current climatic warming, and with several recent records from Norfolk as well as from Essex, further Suffolk sightings seem likely in the not too distant future.

Conservation.

The species is very localised as a British breeder, and populations must be considered as potentially vulnerable to habitat degradation (e.g. from drying out, or from sea-water inundation at coastal sites). As yet, no conservation issues exist in relation to Suffolk.

T. Caroen

Southern Migrant Hawker, male in flight showing the characteristic patterning on the side of the thorax that helps distinguish the species from Migrant Hawker.

SOUTHERN HAWKER
(Blue Hawker)

Aeshna cyanea

S. Plume

Southern Hawker, male. Norfolk, 24th August 2014.

Introduction
Both sexes of the Southern Hawker are large and colourful. Whilst they both have two broad greenish-yellow antehumeral stripes, the male has pairs of green spots on all abdominal segments apart from 9 and 10 where they have blue stripes. The female's colouration is predominantly apple green spots and stripes on a brown background. In flight the male has a distinctive down-turned abdomen and its habit of foraging well away from water make this diagnostic (Emperor has a somewhat similar jizz, but normally stays closer to water). It is inquisitive and will closely investigate any large intruder into its territory – a practice that makes it vulnerable to cats.

Biology
Ovipositing takes place into various plant materials close to the water's edge after the male and female have separated. Material used can include woody matter, moss and both dead and living plant tissue. Occasionally ovipositing takes place directly into the ground. The eggs remain dormant overwinter and the larvae take two or more years to develop.

Emergence is typically from mid-June onwards with the peak flight season being August. In Suffolk, the species has been seen between 3rd June [2005] and 11th November [2005, 2015]. Males are territorial and establish a territory typically along wooded paths and rides. They may be seen typically in the garden towards dusk flying about a metre above the ground.

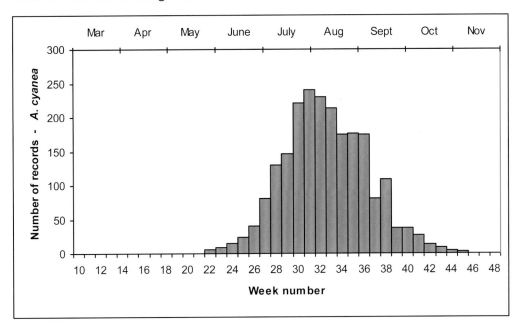

Habitat

The Southern Hawker's preferred habitat is small and medium sized woodland ponds and it is able to tolerate shaded water with well-vegetated edges. This characteristic enables it to colonise urban waters such as park, garden and school ponds, in which it can be a pioneer species, and this has enabled it to significantly increase its distribution. It can also be found in lakes and canals. Adults spend most of their life well away from water and the males will only spend a relatively short time seeking out a receptive female by the water's edge before retiring for a time to their feeding territory and being replaced by another male.

Distribution

Southern Hawkers are essentially a European species, with a few records also from north Africa. They are widespread across Europe, apart from the far north and in some countries surrounding the Mediterranean. In Britain the species is most common in central and southern

Southern Hawker, ovipositing female. Lincs., 9th August 2014.

S. Plume

regions, but has recently extended its range in northern England. Some scattered populations exist in Scotland; these too are expanding.

Southern Hawkers have a wide distribution in Suffolk, but are present in a greater number of tetrads in the east of the county. Mendel reports that the first records of the species in Suffolk were by Paget and Stephens in the 1830s but, in 1992, he was concerned that their numbers might decrease because of the loss of ponds due to both neglect and lowering of the water table. This does not appear to be the case, however, and in the south-east of the county (which has always been well-watched) their distribution has increased markedly. It is only in the north-west, particularly in the Little Ouse catchment area, that this prediction seems to have come about. This area of course is largely Breckland and has a shortage of natural ponds. It is likely that the increasing numbers of garden ponds together with increased farmland pond restoration has allowed increased distribution in many parts of the county.

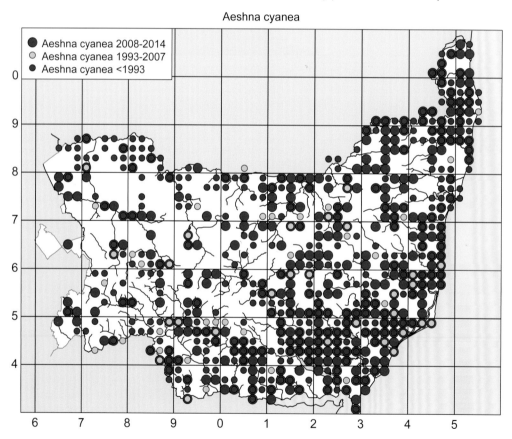

Aeshna cyanea

● Aeshna cyanea 2008-2014
○ Aeshna cyanea 1993-2007
● Aeshna cyanea <1993

Conservation

Southern Hawker is a common and widespread species across the county and no major current conservation issues exist, though the apparent decline in the north-west of the county is perhaps of some concern. The ability of the species to utilise garden ponds means that it is not as susceptible to problems of urbanisation as some Odonata.

BROWN HAWKER   *Aeshna grandis*

Brown Hawker, male. Noar Hill, Hampshire, 23rd August 2007.

Introduction

The Brown Hawker is the only hawker found within the UK to have strongly brown-tinted wings and consequently is perhaps the easiest to identify in flight. Both sexes have two lemon coloured stripes on the side of the thorax and predominantly brown abdomens, with males having blue spots along the sides and females yellow. The Norfolk Hawker, which also has a brown abdomen, has green eyes whereas male Brown Hawkers have blue eyes and females yellow. Norfolk Hawker also has no blue spots, and has clear wings.

Biology

This species is not overly aggressive territorially and can be seen feeding together in considerable numbers on occasion, sometimes well away from water. The female oviposits unaccompanied into dead plant material or emergent vegetation. Softening logs are a favourite site. Eggs remain in diapause until the spring and development takes between two and four years depending on water temperature and food supply. Larvae are active hunters and can prey on flies on the water surface and ovipositing damselflies. Adults too will prey on quite large items. One was seen to take a Ruddy Darter and eat it at one of the pingos at Thompson Common. They emerge over a wide period generally commencing from mid/late June and the flight period continues until October. Extreme first/last dates for Suffolk are currently 20th May [2009] and 30th October [1984].

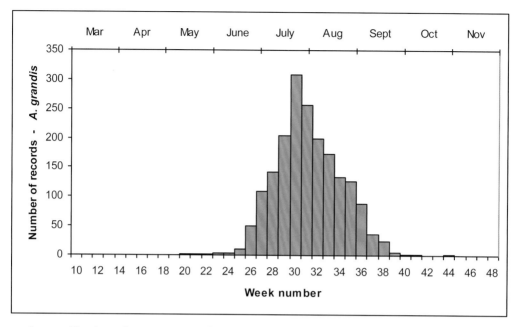

Brown Hawkers have a strong flight, and an interesting observation was made by Toby Abrehart during mid-August 2000 when he discovered an individual some two miles out to sea off Benacre and still flying further away from the coast.

Habitat

This lowland species appears to be able to tolerate higher levels of pollution than most other species and consequently can be found on a wide range of water bodies. Most commonly in Suffolk it is found in grazing dykes, lakes, large ponds and slow-moving rivers although on occasion it will be found on small garden ponds. It requires open areas of water and good marginal vegetation.

Distribution

Within Europe the Brown Hawker ranges from the Alps north as far as the Arctic Circle but is absent from the Iberian peninsula and western France. In Britain it is unaccountably absent from Devon and Cornwall and from West Wales but is relatively common elsewhere within lowland England as far north as County Durham. There is evidence of some range

I. Goodall

Brown Hawker, female. Minsmere, Suffolk, 22nd July 2014.

extension both northwards and westwards and it has also increased its presence along the east coast.

Within Suffolk it was described as *rare* in the early nineteenth century (Paget & Paget, 1834) but *quite common* by the early 20th (Morley, 1911). There has been a significant increase since the Mendel distribution map in 1992. This is most marked along the Waveney and Little Ouse rivers, along the coast from Lowestoft to the Deben, in the Sandlings and in the extreme south of the county. It retains its strong presence in the Fenlands in the north-east.

Breeding within the Arctic Circle, it is clearly able to tolerate low temperatures and therefore we can expect to see continued range extension within the UK.

Aeshna grandis

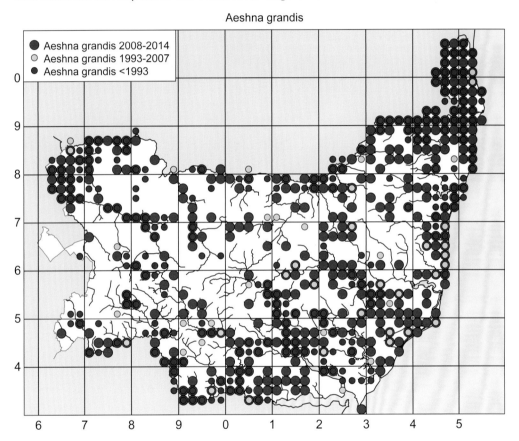

Conservation

The map clearly shows how well the Brown Hawker population is faring in Suffolk. There are no immediate conservation concerns.

66

COMMON HAWKER
(Moorland Hawker)

Aeshna juncea

R. Fairhead

Common Hawker, female. Near Burgh Castle, vice-county of East Suffolk, 28th July 2007.

Introduction

The species is similar in appearance to some other hawkers, most notably the Migrant Hawker. It differs from this in being slightly larger (though this can be difficult to judge in flight), and in having a yellow costa to the forewing. Minor differences in patterning also exist – amongst the most useful being the complete thin yellow thorax stripes seen in male Common Hawker as opposed to the short, partial, stripes seen in Migrant Hawker. Despite being fairly common in parts of northern and western Britain, the species is very scarce in East Anglia, and is only a rare vagrant to Suffolk.

Biology

Females lay their eggs alone, into marginal vegetation. Larval development typically takes two to three years, with the adults emerging in mid-summer. The main flight period for the species is from July to September, though occasional individuals may linger into early November.

Habitat

Common Hawker is primarily a dragonfly of moorlands, breeding principally in acidic pools and lakes and in bogs, though a wider range of habitat is occasionally used (particularly at higher altitudes and latitudes). In Norfolk, the main localities for the species are freshwater pools in coastal dunes, and dykes within grazing marshes – thus being rather different in nature to sites in many other parts of the UK.

Distribution

The species is common in much of northern and central Europe, with only isolated populations, essentially restricted to mountainous areas, in the south and southwest (e.g. in the Pyrenees). It extends eastwards through northern and mid latitude Asia as far as Japan, and also occurs in Canada and some of the northern states of the USA.

Within Britain, records are strongly concentrated towards the north and west, with the main distribution lying north-west of a line roughly from Devon to the Humber. Good, though perhaps declining, populations also exist in the New Forest and the Surrey heaths and environs. In much of south-east England the species is either rare or completely absent. In Suffolk, Mendel (1992) mentions a number of unconfirmed historic records, but notes that these are probably dubious – coming at a time when Migrant Hawker was beginning to establish itself in the county, and observers unfamiliar with either species could have easily made mistakes. Even now, the epithet "common" can lead to misidentification by the unwary. One definite record from the vice-county of East Suffolk is, however, known to exist, when a female was photographed near Burgh Castle on 28th July 2007 (R. Fairhead). Interestingly, there is also an old unconfirmed, but credible, report from this area made in September 1987. The records perhaps relate to dispersing individuals from the small Norfolk population, though immigration from the Continent is also possible.

Conservation

As a rare vagrant to Suffolk – a status that is perhaps unlikely to change in the near future – no immediate conservation issues exist. When considering the long term future of the species in our area, it is however worth emphasising that habitat usage in East Anglia differs from that typical of many other areas in Britain, and unique pressures and requirements may thus be encountered.

MIGRANT HAWKER

Aeshna mixta

S. Plume

Migrant Hawker, two males 'hanging up'. Whitecross Green, Oxfordshire, 3rd August 2014.

Introduction

The male Migrant Hawker has a predominantly blue abdomen and two yellow stripes on either side of the thorax whilst the female is largely brown with yellow spots on the abdomen. Both sexes have a yellow 'nail' mark on the top of the first abdominal section. Confusion with other hawkers is possible but it is smaller than all but the Hairy Dragonfly whose flight period does not usually overlap. Unlike the Southern Hawker, the Migrant Hawker has no green markings and neither is the abdomen held in such a turned down posture in flight. The markings of the Common Hawker are very similar but they have larger antehumeral stripes and a yellow costa, whereas, in common with most British hawkers, the Migrant Hawker's costa is brown.

Biology

The eggs of the Migrant Hawker hatch in the spring and the larva develops rapidly to emerge the same year. This emergence typically commences in mid-July and adults can still be found in November. Extreme first/last dates for Suffolk are currently 28th June [2005] and 26th November [2006]. Adults can sometimes be found feeding communally in large numbers, usually at treetop height. There appears to be little or no aggression between individuals at these gatherings. On occasion numbers can be increased hugely by mass migration. Mendel (1992) quotes such an event observed from a lightship off Lowestoft in 1935. Copulation takes place close to the water's edge and can be extremely lengthy with males being far more tolerant of others than is the case with most other hawkers. Oviposition generally takes place after the pair has separated, and is often into vegetation, such as bulrush, above the water level. Oviposition into mud has also been observed.

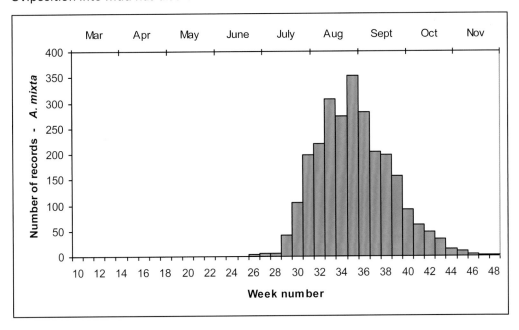

Habitat
Larvae can be found in a wide range of water bodies including both slow-moving rivers and brackish water. Ponds, canals, gravel pits and lakes are also used. The requirement for the larva to develop within one season probably imposes a minimum water temperature require-ment. Well-vegetated fringes to the waterbody with emergent vegetation seem to be important. Open spaces within the conifer woodlands of the Brecks and Sandlings are particularly favoured locally for their mass feeding grounds.

Distribution
The Migrant Hawker is a common European dragonfly occurring throughout southern Europe and into southern Scandinavia; its range extends east to Japan. It was a rarity in Britain until the mid-twentieth century, originally being

Migrant Hawker, mating pair. Boyton, Suffolk.

N. Mason

known as the Scarce Hawker, and was unknown in Ireland until 1997. It appears to still be gradually increasing its range both northwards and westwards within the country, probably driven by climate change. It has now become established in Cumbria and has appeared in Dumfriesshire and a few other Scottish localities. Mendel states that it only became established as a regular Suffolk breeding species following a mass migration in 1935, and believes that reported Common Hawker sightings around this period may in fact have been Migrant Hawkers. The current distribution within the county is similar to that recorded by Mendel (1992) with high densities of records within the Sandlings and Breckland. It is of course possible that this level of sightings along the coastal strip could be influenced by continuing inward migration (Parr, 2015). It is certainly not rare elsewhere within the county and may in fact have increased its presence slightly in the central agricultural belt.

Aeshna mixta

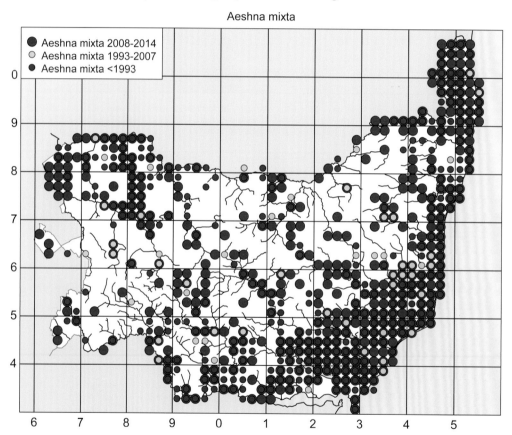

Conservation

Being found in most of the suitable habitat in Suffolk, and the population probably being bolstered by immigration from the Continent, there are no immediate conservation concerns relating to Migrant Hawker.

NORFOLK HAWKER
(Green-eyed Hawker)

Anaciaeshna isosceles

J. Kennerley

Norfolk Hawker, male. Sizewell Belts, Suffolk, 30th June 2013.

Introduction
This species, variously placed in either the genus *Aeshna* or *Anaciaeshna*, is an unmistakeable light-brown hawker with conspicuous green eyes which can be seen from a considerable distance. It has clear wings, with the adults having a yellowish patch at the base of the hindwings. There are two yellow bands on the side of the thorax and a clear yellow triangle (the isosceles) on top of the second abdominal segment.

Biology
In Britain, the Norfolk Hawker has traditionally been associated with Water Soldier *Stratiotes aloides*. The necessity of this association has recently been questioned, as sites for the species (including some in Suffolk) have been discovered which lack the plant, and certainly, on the Continent, there is no such association.

Males can be seen on territorial flights along dykes in grazing marshes, and along the edges of vegetated lakes usually with still water. The females oviposit alone into the leaves and stalks of emerging water plants. The eggs hatch after 3-5 weeks and the larvae normally take two years before emerging. The flight season in Suffolk is from mid-May (the earliest sighting on record is 6th May [1990]) until typically the beginning of August, though there is a record as late as 19th August [1999].

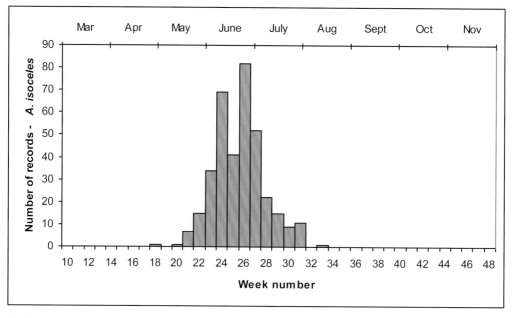

Habitat

Norfolk Hawkers are found in ditches, dykes, ponds and lakes with plenty of marginal vegetation. The ditches are often in grazing marshes where there is good quality water. In north-east Suffolk they are often found where Water Soldier is present, though further south (e.g. Minsmere), this plant may be absent. There is a clear need for emergent vegetation and Broad-leaved Pondweed *Potamogeton natans*, Water Violet *Hottonia palustris*, Frogbit *Hydrocharis morsus-ranae* and Water Milfoil *Myriophyllum* sp. make up typical plant communities where the species is found.

Distribution

This is a European species found as far north as Poland and Denmark, east as far as Turkey but mostly absent from Spain and south-east France. There are dispersed colonies in northern Africa and the Balearic Islands. In Britain Norfolk Hawker has, until recently, only been found in East Anglia, save for the odd occurrence of migrant individuals (e.g. one was photographed at Titchfield Haven, Hampshire, on 26th August 2007). In the last few years, a significant range expansion has, however, occurred. Not only has the species re-colonised Cambridgeshire after an absence of over 100 years, but records are now also regular from parts of east Kent (Cham *et al.*, 2014).

At the time of the last Suffolk Atlas (Mendel, 1992), Norfolk Hawker was well-known from east Norfolk and north-east Suffolk: basically the Norfolk and Suffolk Broads and the Waveney Valley grazing marshes. The Suffolk Wildlife Trust reserves of Castle Marshes and Carlton Marshes were the Suffolk strongholds. However, since 2001 it has also colonised the Minsmere and Sizewell areas and a healthy population now exists in that region. On 13th July 2007 an adult Squacco Heron on the Minsmere Levels was observed to take at least two of these adult dragonflies from rush leaves as it fed stealthily on a dull day.

In the last ten years, other records have come from yet further south in the county, although the status of such individuals is not always clear. One on Sutton Common must have been dispersing, although the species was probably breeding at Hazlewood Marshes before the inundation of December 2013 and subsequent loss of freshwater. Elsewhere, two individuals were seen at Redgrave and Lopham Fen in July 2010.

It is not clear whether the new Minsmere/Sizewell population originated from insects moving south from the Waveney or whether they arrived as migrants over the North Sea. The lack of a strong association with Water Soldier is sometimes taken as evidence for the latter, but this argument is only circumstantial. It is possible that larvae arrived by accidental transportation (as is believed to have been the source of a one-off record, not plotted on the map, from near Lakenheath Fen in late May 1998 (Tunmore, 1999)). It should be noted that the RSPB, however, reports sporadic sightings from Minsmere during the 1980s and even in 1976, suggesting that occasional wanderers have been reaching the area for some while. Perhaps, in time, DNA studies may help provide an insight into the range expansion seen in Suffolk (and indeed elsewhere).

Anaciaeshna isosceles

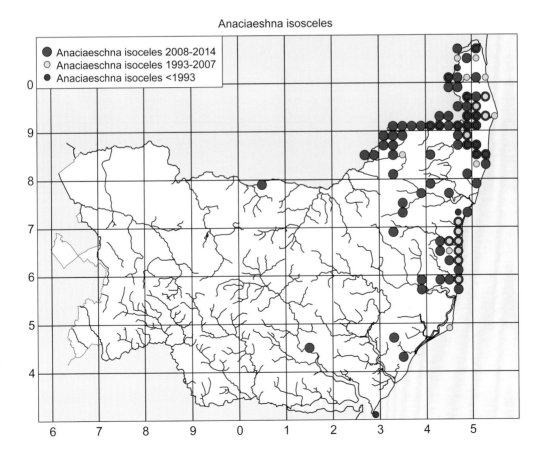

Conservation

Norfolk Hawkers do well where there are clean dykes in grazing marshes. Mendel mentioned that there *"didn't appear to be a change in status but the loss of grazing marsh to arable must have significantly reduced the amount of breeding habitat"*. This was no doubt true, though recent developments have seen the species starting to move out of its old strongholds and into new areas. Hopefully soon the species will spread to suitable habitat around Boyton and Hollesley and even further south into Essex. Clearly conservation organisations must be aware of the need for vegetated dykes and should not clear them out too often or too thoroughly. In addition, many already-established populations are found in areas that are very low-lying and hence potentially vulnerable to inundation with sea water due to surge events and to possible longer-term changes in sea level. Efforts to minimise the impact of such phenomena are thus to be encouraged, where feasible. Fortunately the recent range expansions of Norfolk Hawker within Britain mean that not all populations are now, however, within such low-lying areas.

R. Fairhead

Norfolk Hawker, male. Waveney Forest, Suffolk, 25th June 2009.

VAGRANT EMPEROR
Anax ephippiger

Vagrant Emperor, male. Great Yarmouth, Norfolk, 4th October 2011.

Introduction
The Vagrant Emperor is a medium-large dragonfly, slightly smaller than many of the other hawkers. Mature males are sandy brown with a blue or violet saddle-shaped patch at the base of the abdomen. Females are generally more uniform, with a much less obvious 'saddle', though occasionally this may be nearly as pronounced as in males. The species is superficially similar to Lesser Emperor, but is distinguished by a variety of features including the smaller size, paler brown body colour, and brown rather than green eyes.

Biology
The Vagrant Emperor is a strongly migratory/nomadic species, with a short larval duration but long adult life. Oviposition is typically while still in tandem; the eggs and larvae develop rapidly and in its tropical strongholds adults can emerge after a few weeks. Even in central Europe, migrants arriving in spring can produce a second generation the same year (Maibach *et al.*, 1989). Breeding attempts have occasionally been reported in Britain, but none has apparently proved successful. The species is known to be active at night, and has been caught in UV moth traps on a number of occasions (Parr, 2011).

Habitat

The species breeds in shallow, warm, pools and lakes that may even be ephemeral in nature. On migration, individuals may be observed in a considerable variety of habitats

Distribution

The species has its centre of distribution in tropical parts of Africa and southwest Asia, wandering with the winds to breed following seasonal rains. Normally individuals remain within the Intertropical Convergence Zone, but given appropriate local weather conditions they may break out and reach quite high latitudes. Breeding is probably annual in the Mediterranean region, and the species currently occurs nearly annually in Britain (though it used to be less common). Sporadic records have even come from as far north as the Faroe Islands and Iceland, where it is the only species of dragonfly that has been recorded. Vagrant individuals have also been observed in the Caribbean; indeed the species may now even be starting to breed in the region.

Within Britain, records are widespread, as would be expected from a strong migrant. There is, however, both a southerly, and a coastal, bias to sightings. Records have become more frequent in Britain and nearby areas of north-west Europe over the last decade or two, and while some of this may simply reflect an increasing number of observers, there is a suggestion that at least part of the increase is real. The only records from Suffolk relate to two (different?) individuals seen in the Lowestoft area during early October 2013, though one was also seen just over the county boundary in Great Yarmouth during October 2011.

Conservation

Being a rare vagrant to the county, no relevant conservation issues exist. Attempted breeding has occasionally been reported in Britain (e.g. Parr, 2011) but is not thought to have been successful. Any progeny that might result will also be migratory, so that even successful breeding will not lead to the establishment of permanent British populations.

EMPEROR DRAGONFLY
(Blue Emperor)

Anax imperator

M. Holland

Emperor Dragonfly, ovipositing female being buzzed by a male Common Blue Damselfly. Suffolk, 22nd August, 2012.

Introduction

The apple green thorax and the longitudinally dark striped, sky blue abdomen make the male Emperor Dragonfly unmistakeable. However, since it spends most of its time aggressively patrolling its territory over water, it is often only viewed in silhouette. Its down-turned abdomen makes this similar to that of the Southern Hawker but this latter species spends far more time over land. The female has a similarly coloured, large thorax and its abdomen has a much broader brown stripe with a dull green background colour.

Biology

Synchronised emergence usually occurs in early June (the earliest Suffolk record of adults being as early as 13th May [2010]) and an exceptionally long flight period continues well into August, with occasional individuals sometimes being seen even later (the latest record for Suffolk being 27th September [2009]). Larvae usually take two years to mature but, in warm water with an excellent food supply, may emerge after one year in which case they create a second instalment of emergence. The male strongly defends its territory which he patrols vigorously. Mating lasts about ten minutes and after separation females oviposit into floating vegetation, moving from one plant to another rapidly. The eggs hatch after around three weeks and larvae enter diapause in the late summer or early autumn.

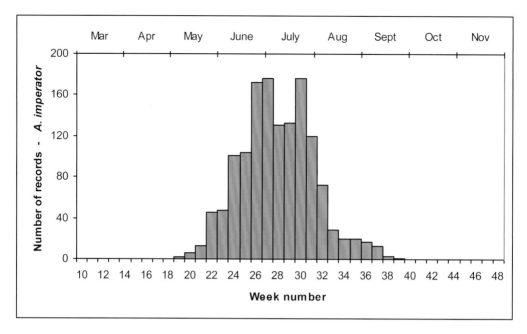

Being a large insect there are several examples of Emperors predating other species. They have been noted taking Four-spot Chaser, White Admiral butterfly and moth species including Clouded Buff and Large Yellow Underwing. They are often recorded hunting over Lower Hollesley Common in July where the most obvious prey species would be Silver-studded Blue butterflies.

Habitat

Emperors tolerate a wide range of habitats from garden ponds to large bodies of still or slow-moving water and, on occasion, brackish environments. It prefers sites with rich marginal vegetation, thick mats of floating pondweeds for oviposition, and areas of open water but it will also colonise newly created ponds and reservoirs as a pioneer species.

Distribution

The Emperor dragonfly is a very widespread species, occurring in much of Africa and western Eurasia. It is found throughout Europe as far north as Denmark and southern Sweden, though it is currently expanding northwards. In the UK it is predominantly a southern species but has also spread northwards

R. Fairhead

Emperor Dragonfly, emergent. Bradwell, Norfolk, 11th June 2013.

surprisingly rapidly in the last few years and is now even possibly established in some parts of southern Scotland. Its story in Suffolk is similar. Mendel tells us that the first record of an Emperor here was as recent as 1943 and that its numbers increased during the period of the previous Atlas (1980–1992), following the exceptionally hot summers of 1989 and 1990. That increase has clearly continued apace and the current distribution chart shows that this species has been recorded in almost four times as many 2km squares as that survey. It is particularly widespread in the south-east but can now be found across the county. It probably now occupies most of the suitable water bodies in Suffolk.

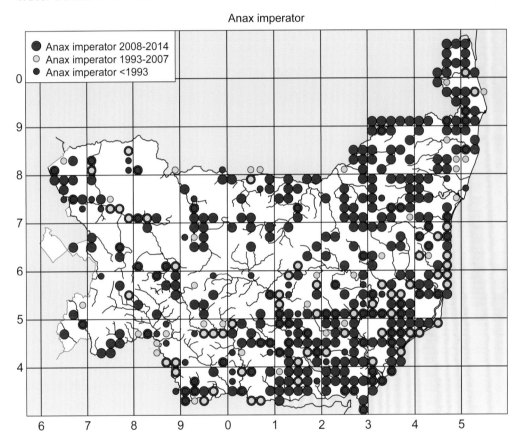

Anax imperator

● Anax imperator 2008-2014
○ Anax imperator 1993-2007
● Anax imperator <1993

Conservation

It is thought that the increase in distribution is as a result of climate change, although whether this is caused by higher air temperatures during the flight season or higher water temperatures during the winter is uncertain. Increases in this species are more likely to be real, and not due to surveyor bias or the insect being missed, because it is such an obvious species. It therefore seems reasonable to predict that, subject to there not being a prolonged period of colder weather, the Emperor Dragonfly will continue to be one of Suffolk's most common and spectacular Odonata species.

LESSER EMPEROR   *Anax parthenope*

D. Dana

Lesser Emperor, male. Combley Lakes, Isle of Wight, 25th July 2012.

Introduction

The Lesser Emperor is a large dragonfly, only slightly smaller than Emperor Dragonfly. Males are dark olive-brown in appearance with bright green eyes and a prominent blue saddle at the base of the abdomen that is larger than that shown by male Vagrant Emperor. Females are typically very drab apart from their greenish eyes, though a blue form exists that has quite a lot of blue on the abdomen (a similar form is also occasionally seen in males). The species is best separated from Emperor Dragonfly by the brown, rather than green, thorax and from Vagrant Emperor by the greenish rather than brown eyes and by the generally darker appearance. Male Migrant Hawkers are also a possible source of confusion, due to their prominent blue flashes at the base of the abdomen.

Biology

The species is one of the few hawker-type dragonflies that oviposit in tandem. Eggs are laid into plants or mud, and larval development typically takes two years, though it may perhaps be more rapid when conditions are particularly favourable. The species is a notable migrant, but resident populations are also found in southern Europe and elsewhere; factors influencing the balance between these two life-styles are poorly understood. In Britain, most individuals appear to be primary immigrants, but locally-bred individuals also occur as a result of successful breeding attempts. Few, if any, stable breeding colonies are however known. The flight season is between May and early September, with occasional records into October.

Habitat
Lesser Emperor is a generalist species, frequenting a range of water bodies including ponds, lakes and slower-flowing rivers. In Britain there is perhaps a tendency for the species to be noted at larger waters, but this is by no means absolute.

Distribution
The species occurs from North Africa and western Europe right across to Japan, though the Asian subspecies *A.p. julius* (sometimes treated as a distinct species) has a green thorax that results in a somewhat different appearance. In Europe the species is most common in southern regions, but occurs as a migrant further north. Recent years have seen a significant northwards range expansion (Parr *et al.*, 2004), with sightings having now even been made in Latvia and southern Sweden (Mitra, 2013).

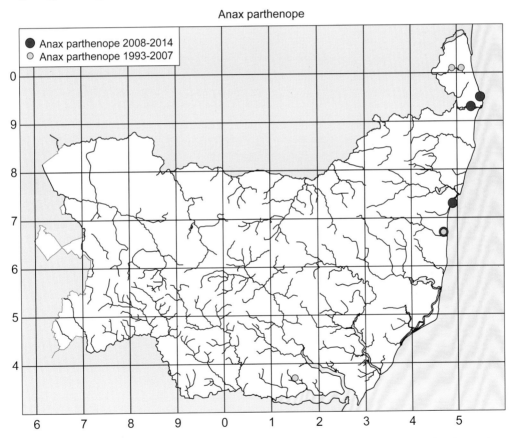

Anax parthenope

In Britain, the first confirmed record occurred in 1996 (Phillips, 1997). Since then, records have become more regular, and sightings are now made at an average of roughly 20+ localities each year. Sightings have been spread over much of England

and south Wales, with one additional report as far north as the Shetland Isles (Cham *et al.*, 2014); several records have also been forthcoming from Ireland since the year 2000. Most British individuals are clearly migrants, but successful breeding has been proven in Cornwall and Kent, and has no doubt also occurred elsewhere from time to time.

In Suffolk the species was unknown at the time of Mendel (1992). In the last 10–15 years there have, however, been occasional records from coastal and near coastal sites such as Minsmere and Lound Lakes, the latter site indeed seeing records in both 2003 and 2007. Inland records are perhaps soon to be forthcoming, particularly if the species continues to become more common.

Conservation

As an irregular immigrant to Suffolk, no conservation issues presently exist. The species seems to be slow in establishing a foothold as a British breeder, possibly because of intrinsic dispersive tendencies that might make any locally-bred individuals move away from their natal sites, rather than remaining around to establish colonies.

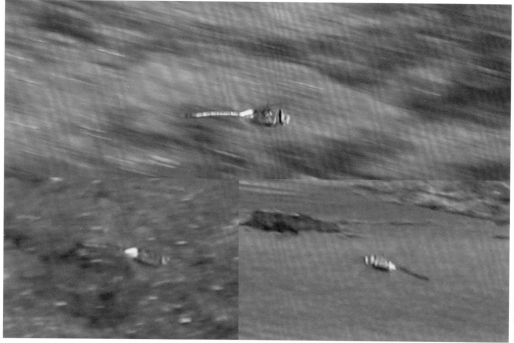

A. Easton

'Record shots' of male Lesser Emperor. Lound, Suffolk, July 2003.

HAIRY DRAGONFLY
(Hairy Hawker)

Brachytron pratense

J. Kennerley

Hairy Dragonfly, male. Newbourne Springs, Suffolk, 6th June 2013.

Introduction

The Hairy Dragonfly is one of the smaller hawkers, being roughly 60mm in length. Males have a dark background colour with extensive greenish markings on the thorax and paired blue spots on the abdomen, while in the female the markings are smaller and yellow in colour. The thorax is quite hairy, which gives the species its vernacular name, but this is generally not obvious in the field. The main distinguishing feature of Hairy Dragonfly is its early flight period – the species being one of the very first Odonata to emerge in spring. This makes confusion with other hawkers unlikely.

Biology

Oviposition takes place into floating dead and decaying plant material, and larvae are also usually found clinging to fragments of floating plant debris. Larval development is slow, and adults do not typically emerge until the second or even third year after the eggs were laid. The Hairy Dragonfly emerges early in the season, towards the end of April, and the flight period lasts until early July. Current extreme first/last dates for Suffolk are 18th April [2007] and 11th July [2010].

R. Fairhead

Hairy Dragonfly, female. Belton, Norfolk, 27th May 2013.

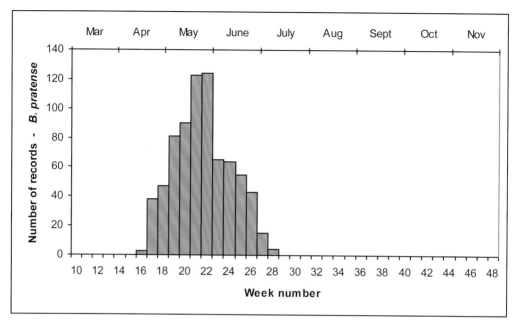

Habitat

The species favours standing or slow-flowing waters with rich open and well-structured marginal vegetation, including sites such as canals, slow-flowing rivers, dykes on grazing marshes, and some well-vegetated lakes and ponds. The presence of floating plant material is important for the species, but most sites also have extensive areas of open water. Many sites for Hairy Dragonfly are associated with stands of trees that provide shelter, and in which adults may feed. The species is however also at home in the open landscapes of grazing marshes.

Distribution

Hairy Dragonfly is found throughout much of Europe (occurring as far east as the Urals), but is absent from the far north, and rather scarce and patchily distributed in the far south, with very few records from Iberia. In Ireland the species is widespread, whereas in Britain it is predominantly southern in distribution, there being rather few sites known from northern England and Scotland. Its range does, however, appear to be spreading, with many new localities discovered in e.g. East Anglia and the East Midlands over the last 20 years.

In Suffolk, the Hairy Dragonfly used to be essentially restricted to the grazing marshes of the coastal strip, a feature that was not uncommon elsewhere in

Hairy Dragonfly, male, being eaten by a Fen Raft Spider *Dolomedes plantarius*. Castle Marshes, Suffolk, 20th June 2014.

Britain during the last century. Mendel (1992) also mentioned sightings from Redgrave and Lopham Fen, although all precisely localised records came from the Norfolk side of the county border. Since the work of Mendel (1992), the species has, however, expanded its range within the county quite considerably. It is now found well inland along most of the major river valleys, and in the last 15 years populations have even been discovered at several sites in west Suffolk. These include the Lakenheath Fen area and the mid-Stour river valley. More isolated inland sites also exist at Lackford Lakes SWT Reserve and nearby Dale Pond (situated in The King's Forest), as well as in the grounds of Ickworth House, Horringer.

Brachytron pratense

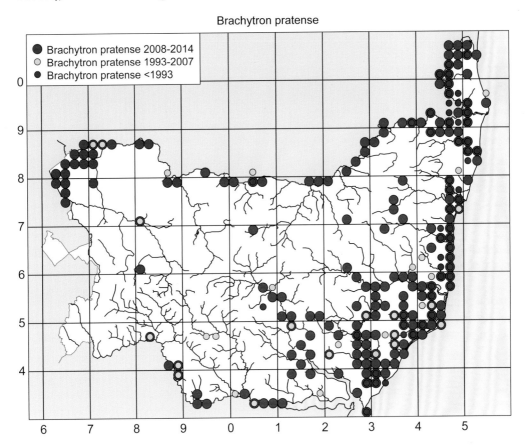

Legend:
● Brachytron pratense 2008-2014
○ Brachytron pratense 1993-2007
● Brachytron pratense <1993

Conservation

Hairy Dragonfly is categorised as of Least Concern in the Odonata Red Data List for Great Britain. Showing a strong association with river valleys and grazing marshes within the county, the dragonfly is potentially vulnerable to pollution and to insensitive management regimes. However, with a strongly positive trend in local and national population levels, there appears to be no major current threat to the species.

DOWNY EMERALD   *Cordulia aenea*

P. Hunt

Downy Emerald, male. Clamerkin, Isle of Wight, 5th June 2014.

Introduction

We do not currently have any emerald dragonflies in Suffolk, though the Downy Emerald was once present in the county, and may conceivably reappear one day. Downy Emerald is a dark green medium-sized insect with the male having a club-shaped abdomen. They fly fast along the edge of pools and lakes, occasionally hovering, resembling a helicopter. The male has dark-brown patches at the base of the wings. Females have yellow and white patches on the underside of the abdomen.

Biology

The females are only seen at water when they are ready to mate. Otherwise they feed and mature in nearby woodland rides and clearings. The males are very territorial, patrolling their water body for long periods of time, flying fast about one metre above the surface. They also will fly off to feed in woodland. The females oviposit alone and the larvae take two or three years before they emerge. This species can tolerate coolish waters. The flight season is from mid-April to the end of July.

Habitat

Downy Emeralds breed in still water ponds and lakes, often quite open but with nearby woodland. They may use gravel pits, canals and fishing lakes. The larvae need plenty of plant material on the bottom of the water body. Rushes and sedges are used for the larvae to emerge, the presence of exuviae being the only proof of breeding at some sites.

Distribution

Downy Emeralds occur over much of northern Eurasia. They are found in central and northern Europe including much of France, Germany, The Netherlands, southern Sweden and Finland. In Britain the main centre of distribution is Dorset, Hampshire, Berkshire, Surrey, Sussex and Kent. There are scattered populations in parts of Wales and areas including Somerset, Cumbria and western Scotland. There is presently a strong local population in Bedfordshire and it is also found in eastern Norfolk with isolated populations in Essex and Cambridgeshire.

In Suffolk the only confirmed breeding sites were in the Huntingfield-Heveningham area, where they were present in the nineteenth century and still there in 1943 (Mendel, 1992). The Norfolk population has shown some signs of expanding. There are a number of sites in Suffolk which this species could colonise and some of us probably fantasise of such events when surveying them!

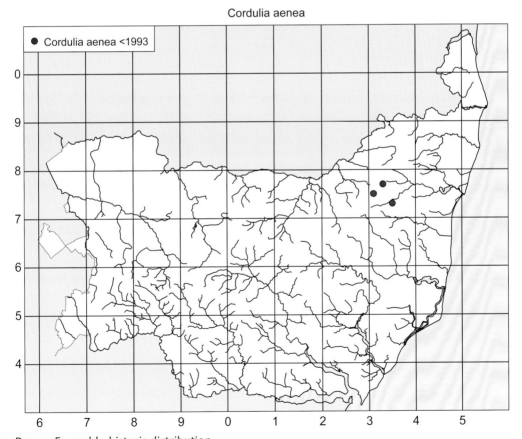

Cordulia aenea

● Cordulia aenea <1993

Downy Emerald - historic distribution

WHITE-FACED DARTER sp.   *Leucorrhinia* sp.

Mendel (1992) described the discovery of at least three dragonflies at Westwood Marshes, Walberswick, during late May to mid-June 1992 that were ascribed to the White-faced Darter *Leucorrhinia dubia*. No further sightings were made after this period, and it is likely that the individuals were migrants.

White-faced Darter is a species typically associated with acidic bog pools that support *Sphagnum* moss. It is found in central and northern Europe east across Siberia, with isolated breeding populations in France and also in Britain, where it is relatively widespread in northern Scotland, but extremely local further south. The only previous records from East Anglia relate to a small population apparently present in the Epping area of Essex in the mid-nineteenth century, but long since extinct. Slightly further afield, populations were still present in the Thursley area of the Surrey Heaths at the time of Mendel (1992), but these were in decline and indeed are also now extinct (the last records apparently coming in 1999). Although there is circumstantial evidence on the Continent that the species may wander a little, it is not a recognised strong migrant and this fact, plus the absence of any particularly close British populations during the 1990s, means the occurrence of White-faced Darters on the Suffolk coast is somewhat unexpected.

In Europe, the genus *Leucorrhinia* is represented by no less than five species, and it is conceivable that the 1992 Suffolk records may actually refer to a species other than *L. dubia*. While many of the other species are relatively distinctive, the Northern (or Ruby) White-faced Darter *L. rubicunda* is quite similar in appearance to White-faced Darter. This is especially true in the case of males. The species also has known migratory tendencies (Parr, 2013), and while its preferred habitat is similar to that of White-faced Darter, it also occasionally breeds in more nutrient-rich, well-vegetated habitats similar to where it was found in Suffolk. The possibility therefore exists that the Walberswick individuals were not White-faced Darter, but were in fact Northern White-faced Darter. This is relatively widespread in parts of Northern Europe, and breeds as close to Britain as The Netherlands.

Mendel (1992) mentions that a photograph was taken of the male seen at Walberswick on 24th May 1992. Unfortunately it has proved impossible to locate this, but efforts to do so are continuing. In the future, the identity of the Walberswick white-faced darters may thus finally be resolved. It is worth noting that since the time of Mendel (1992), confirmed records of Large White-faced Darter *L. pectoralis* have also been made on the Suffolk coast (see the following species account).

LARGE WHITE-FACED DARTER
(Yellow-spotted Whiteface)

Leucorrhinia pectoralis

E. Beaumont

Large White-faced Darter, male. Docwra's Ditch, Dunwich Heath, Suffolk, 16th June 2012.

Introduction
Large White-faced Darter is currently only a rare vagrant to Britain. The species is similar in appearance to, though slightly larger than, White-faced Darter, showing a prominent white frons (face) in both sexes. Females and immature males have yellow spotting on the abdomen, while in mature males many of these spots turn red. The spot on abdominal segment S7 however remains yellow, giving individuals a rather characteristic appearance. Females can be told from White-faced Darter by their larger yellow abdominal spots.

Biology
Females oviposit either alone, or with a guarding male nearby; eggs are deposited onto the water surface. The larvae overwinter twice, with emergence then taking place in spring. The species is a relatively early flier, and adults are primarily on the wing during late May and June. Individuals are known to show dispersive/migratory tendencies under some conditions, particularly when local population levels are high, and sightings may thus occur outside the species' normal range (Parr, 2013).

Habitat
This species has a somewhat broader habitat preference than White-faced Darter. It favours clear waters with floating plants and well-developed marginal vegetation and can, on the Continent, thus be found breeding in marshes, fenlands and well-

vegetated forest lakes in addition to peatlands. In Suffolk, an individual settled for some days by a fresh-water coastal dyke flowing slowly towards the sea, with plenty of reeds and rushes on the edges and large floating mats of Marsh St. John's Wort *Hypericum elodes* (Beaumont and Beaumont, 2012). Migrating individuals may appear in a greater range of habitats.

Distribution

The main range of the species covers the area from western Siberia to central Europe, reaching as far west as The Netherlands and parts of France. It has a somewhat more southerly distribution than other European white-faced darter species, occurring only in southern Scandinavia, and having isolated populations as far south as the Balkans. Until very recently, the sole British record related to a specimen taken *"near Sheerness, Kent"* sometime during June 1859. The exact locality is unknown, but is believed by some to have been on board a boat in the Thames Estuary (Lucas, 1900). However, in 2012 two separate mature males turned up on the Suffolk coast: one at Landguard on 27th May, and another at Docwra's Ditch, Dunwich Heath, over 16th to 19th June. These individuals were apparently part of a large and dramatic mixed movement of Large White-faced Darter, Northern (or Ruby) White-faced Darter *L. rubicunda*, and Four-spotted Chasers that took place in western Europe during spring 2012 (Parr, 2013).

Conservation

As a vagrant to Suffolk (and Britain), no specific conservation issues exist – though it is listed on Annexes II and IV of the EU Habitats Directive by virtue of past declines in parts of its European range. There has, however, been something of a recovery in recent years and with the species likely to benefit from climate change (Jaeschke *et al.*, 2013) it is conceivable that British records will become more frequent.

G. Švitra

Large White-faced Darter, female.

BROAD-BODIED CHASER *Libellula depressa*

Broad-bodied Chaser, male. Woodbridge, Suffolk, 5th June 2010.

Introduction
The very plump, flattened abdomen is characteristic of the insect. Both sexes have pale blue, thin ante-humeral stripes and brown eyes. All the wing bases are very dark brown. The males quickly develop a blue pruinescence on the abdomen with yellow spots along the segment sides. Females are a golden brown on the abdomen, again with yellow spots at the margins.

Biology
The insect is typically on the wing from late April/early May and a few tatty individuals are still around in late-July; occasional fresher-looking late individuals may represent a second phase of emergence. In Suffolk, adults have been noted between 25th April [2011] and 2nd October [1942]. The species is never plentiful, with suitable small ponds attracting maybe one or two individuals at any one time. However, they are great wanderers and will fly along hedgerows and in woodland in search of new waters to colonise. Mendel (1992) considered the dragonfly to be a partial migrant and said that the evidence suggested that in Suffolk *"the Broad-bodied Chaser survives for long periods at low population levels, becoming more common at irregular intervals as a result of immigration"*. There was no evidence of mass immigrations during the 2008–2014 survey. Among the records of predation on Broad-bodied Chasers are individuals being taken by hornets (quite a task), and the ambitious Wren *Troglodytes troglodytes*, shown on BBC TV (Springwatch 2015), which eventually managed to feed its chicks with the body of a Broad-bodied Chaser after making several attempts!

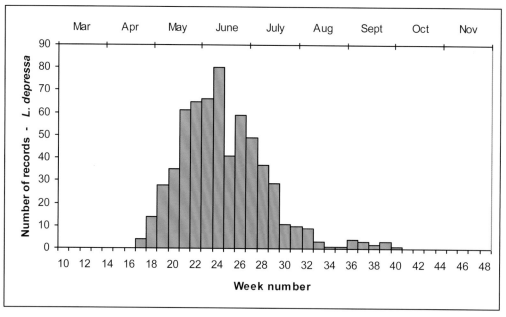

Habitat

This dragonfly favours sunny, bare, shallow waters and will colonise the smallest of ponds; in consequence is often seen in gardens where females and immatures can be mistaken by gardeners as hornets. It is often the first dragonfly to colonise new ponds. It generally avoids rivers, but is frequently found on adjacent dyke systems. It has the habit of regularly returning to the same low perch after swift flights along the pond margins. A good example of colonisation of small ponds was seen at Landguard Point where there is little standing fresh water. There were no records for the site prior to 1998, but singles in 2004 and 2008 then led to almost annual occurrences, including emergences noted in 2014, from a flooded gun emplacement maintained as a pond by Landguard Bird Observatory.

Distribution

Broad-bodied Chaser is one of the most common dragonfly species throughout Europe, and its range extends to central Asia. It is widespread and common throughout southern England and Wales, and has recently been expanding northwards with the first Scottish record coming in 2003. The Broad-bodied Chaser is widely distributed throughout Suffolk and is absent only from the extreme west of the county, where suitable waterbodies are scarce. Populations are sparse in drier Breckland localities and the intensively farmed areas of central Suffolk, but are plentiful in the Suffolk

Broad-bodied Chaser, female. Pakenham, Suffolk, 28th June 2014.

S. Plume

Sandlings. Mendel (1992) thought that it was *"most frequent across the boulder clay area of central Suffolk"* although the current distribution map does not present quite the same picture. The concentration of records to the east of Ipswich and in the Sandlings possibly reflects the presence of numerous dragonfly recorders in these regions.

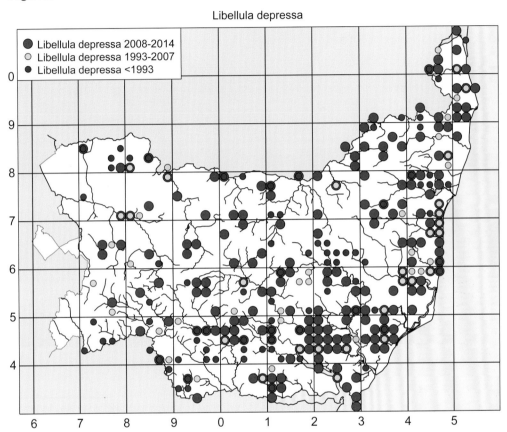

Libellula depressa

The Broad-bodied Chaser has a chequered history in Suffolk. There were few records prior to the 1940s but thereafter records and comments indicate that it became plentiful during that decade (Mendel, 1992). It was scarce in the 1980s and its presence in Suffolk Breckland was not noted until 1990 and 1991. Its range has expanded northwards in the UK and it has consolidated its range in Suffolk between the survey years, the species now being found in 22 new 10-km squares. There has been a significant increase in populations which have run parallel with the consolidation of its range.

Conservation
Although fairly widespread, Broad-bodied Chaser requires small pools that are unpolluted and not too overgrown. The continued improvement of the water quality in most of Suffolk could improve the spread of this species. The clearing and restoration of farm and garden ponds, especially where they have been lost in central Suffolk, could well improve the number of sites where this species is found.

SCARCE CHASER
(Blue Chaser)

Libellula fulva

R. Fairhead

Scarce Chaser, immature male. Castle Marshes, Suffolk, 5th June 2005.

Description

The sexes of teneral Scarce Chasers look very similar and soon develop to show a distinctive vivid orange colouration, black triangular shaped markings on the upper surface of each abdominal section and dark bases to the hindwings. The males obtain the pale blue pruinescence on the abdomen when reaching maturity. Blackish marks on either side of the mature male's body are caused by wearing of the blue pruinescence as the female clings on during copulation. Males have blue eyes.

Biology

Ovipositing takes place in slow-moving rivers and then the eggs lie embedded in the mud of the riverbed. Larval development usually takes two years. The insect has a relatively short flight season; synchronised emergence usually begins around mid-May, and adults can be seen on the wing until mid-July, during which time they mate and lay eggs to complete the cycle. Extreme first/last dates for Suffolk are 9th May [2011] and 7th August [1987]. Ovipositing females require areas of slow-flowing open water, and the adults require some shrub or tree shelter.

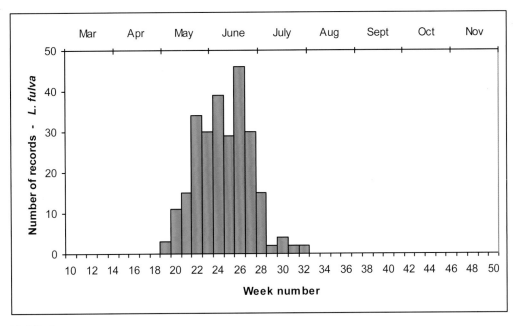

Habitat

The Scarce Chaser is a species of lowland river floodplains and usually inhabits slow-flowing, meandering rivers and the associated dyke systems. Suffolk rivers are ideal for this dragonfly, but it also patrols nearby gravel pits and ponds, although breeding has yet to be confirmed at these sites. For example, at Mutford it is found almost annually around farm ponds that are two kilometres from its Waveney Valley stronghold. Inhabited sites characteristically have good water quality, which supports submerged and floating plants as well as prolific stands of emergent vegetation.

Distribution

The Scarce Chaser is widespread, but rather local, over much of southern and central Europe, It extends as far north as southern Finland, and east to the Caspian Sea. In Britain the species was traditionally restricted to six main regions: the Norfolk/Suffolk border, West Sussex, Wiltshire/Somerset, Cambridgeshire, Kent and Dorset/Hampshire. In recent decades, there has however been significant range expansion, most notably into Devon and the West Midlands.

Within Suffolk, the Scarce Chaser's presence in the Shipmeadow/Fritton area has been well documented, but its true distribution was not realised until fieldwork for the original Suffolk Dragonfly Survey (Mendel, 1992) was completed. Its stronghold was then confined to the lower stretches of the River Waveney, i.e. part of the Norfolk/Suffolk Broads population, but did not extend beyond the navigable stretches of the river that ended at Shipmeadow. Since that time it has, however, expanded dramatically westwards and now frequents a further 10 kilometres upstream in the River Waveney. It has also colonised several other river catchments. The population on the Stour has been known since 1997 but those on the Gipping, and on the Little Ouse and Lark in the north-west of the county, were only found during the current Atlas survey.

Libellula fulva

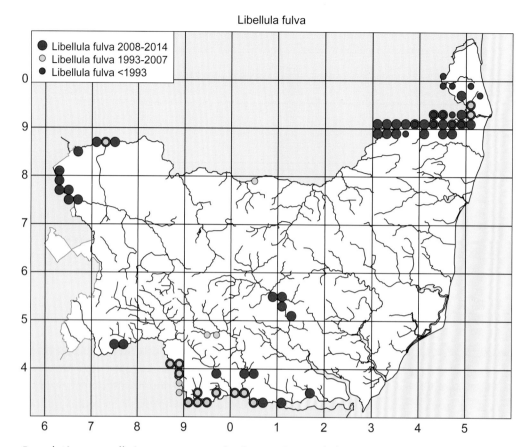

- Libellula fulva 2008-2014
- Libellula fulva 1993-2007
- Libellula fulva <1993

Populations on all rivers appear to be increasing and the insect is likely to consolidate its range to colonise other river systems in Suffolk. The dragonfly is now present in 13 new 10-km squares and the trends suggest that it is likely to further expand its range in coming decades.

Conservation

Although increasing, *L. fulva* is still quite restricted in distribution within Britain and is presently listed under category 3 (Scarce) in the British Red Data Book on Insects. General management principles should include maintaining inhabited sites and the adjacent landscape, controlling water quality and managing boating activity and unofficial mooring in sensitive areas. There should also be best practice guidelines for managing inhabited sites, particularly regarding dredging, management of aquatic vegetation and scrub control. The strong positive trend of Suffolk and national populations however mean that the species' future looks promising.

FOUR-SPOTTED CHASER
Libellula quadrimaculata

J. Richardson

Four-spotted Chaser, female. Eastbridge, Suffolk, 9th July 2015.

Description

In flight, this uniformly-brown dragonfly is not that distinctive. However, the presence of four dark spots, one half-way along the leading edge of each wing, is a diagnostic feature and gives the insect its name. The sexes are alike with a brown abdomen becoming darker towards the rear, a brown thorax and brown eyes. There is a row of yellow spots along each side of the abdomen. The hind-wing bases are also very dark and a colour form *praenubila* has a general darkening of the wing tips, along with an enlargement of the four wing-spots. The amber in the wing bases can sometimes be quite extensive and catches the eye.

Biology

The number of patrolling adults present is normally in single figures, but counts of 100 or more can be noted on larger areas of standing water. The flight season is mid-April to mid-August (Suffolk records spanning the period 22nd April [2011] to 21st August [1987]), the larvae having taken two years to develop. Adults are quite active in late spring and summer, frequently perching on tall stems amongst marginal vegetation around ponds of all sizes. The species is often one of the first dragonflies to colonise new ponds. Individuals are extremely territorial and will aggressively chase off potential invaders. However, the insect can also be prone to predation as seen at Bures during the current survey, when an Emperor Dragonfly was seen to seize a Four-spot Chaser on the wing, take it to the bank, kill it and drop it into the water. They are also commonly taken by Hobbies, a sight seen at Minsmere and Lakenheath Fen.

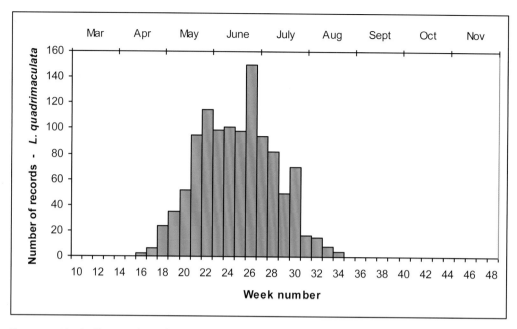

Four-spotted Chaser is a known migrant and in the past has shown some huge movements, particularly on the Continent (with flocks sometimes into the millions), though major arrivals have also been noted in parts of Britain on occasion (Cham *et al.*, 2014). In recent times, migration has however appeared much more low-key. It does however still occur; small numbers for instance arrived at Landguard at the time when Britain's second-ever Large White-faced Darter was recorded there at the end of May 2012. Small-scale arrivals are likely still regular, but frequently go un-noticed.

Habitat

Four-spotted Chaser is found at the margins of shallow ponds and lakes which have well-developed emergent vegetation and some open water; such waterbodies may be neutral or acidic. It often frequents the dykes and open water in reed-beds.

Four-spotted Chaser, female ovipositing. Lackford Lakes, Suffolk, 22nd June 2010.

I. Goodall

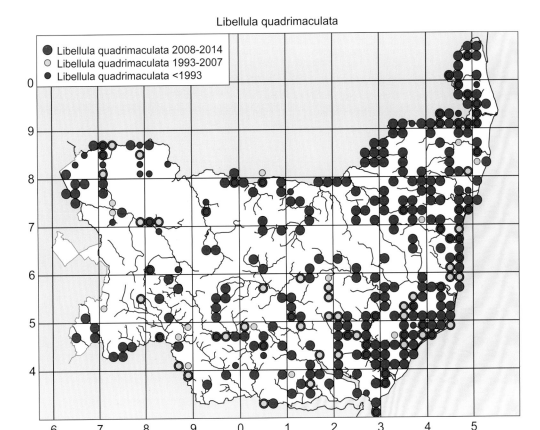

Libellula quadrimaculata

Legend:
- Libellula quadrimaculata 2008-2014
- Libellula quadrimaculata 1993-2007
- Libellula quadrimaculata <1993

Distribution

The species is widespread and abundant across temperate Eurasia and North America, and is common throughout virtually all of the British Isles. It is presently widespread in Suffolk although there is a bias to the coast and river catchments towards the east of the county.

Historically, it would seem that the Four-spotted Chaser used to be relatively rare and local within Suffolk, with its strongholds in the Waveney broads area. By the time of Mendel (1992), records were, however, increasing and its distribution starting to spread. This increase has continued since the 1980–1992 survey, and the insect has now been recorded from a further 27 new 10-km squares. The apparent expansion reflects the general increase shown in the national Atlas, and may be due to a combination of factors including immigration, habitat changes and improved water quality, as well as to greater surveyor effort.

Conservation

Four-spotted Chaser is now widespread throughout Suffolk and is a good coloniser. There are no particular conservation concerns.

BLACK-TAILED SKIMMER   *Orthetrum cancellatum*

M. Holland

Black-tailed Skimmer, male. Suffolk, 7th July 2014.

Introduction
This is the only skimmer found in Suffolk at present, although Keeled Skimmer is a possible coloniser in the future. Black-tailed Skimmer is a medium-sized dragonfly; the adult male can initially be mistaken for male chasers but the wings are completely clear, having none of the brown patches in the hind wings shown by chaser dragonflies. Whilst the abdomen of mature males is blue with pruinescence, and the black tail, the females and immature males are yellowish with a black ladder-like pattern down the abdomen. In the mature insect, the eyes are greenish brown in females, and dark greenish blue in males. Sometimes the tell-tale signs of the male having mated can be seen where the pruinescence has been scraped off by a clinging female. As its name suggests, the species flies quite low over the edge of still water bodies and is usually seen perched on the ground. They are often first seen when they rise from their resting place on the ground in front of you.

Biology
Black-tailed Skimmers are typically on the wing from the end of May until the end of August, rarely even later (very late records perhaps represent a second phase of emergence). In Suffolk, the extreme first/last dates are currently 17th May [2011] and 2nd October [1997]. The male can be seen being territorial on the edges of open water bodies, often perching on bare soil, rocks or tree roots. They normally return to the same spot to perch. Females usually only return to the water to breed. Eggs are typically laid in shallow water, the female dipping into the water surface, with the male often guarding. In Suffolk the larvae usually take two years to develop. The species has been known to tolerate brackish conditions.

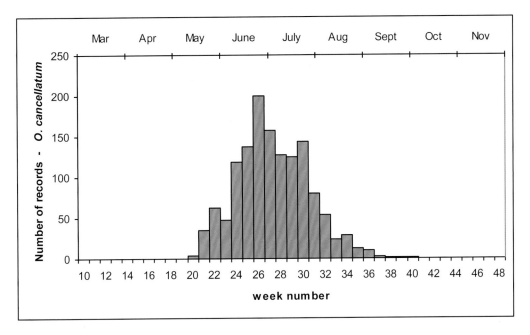

Habitat

Black-tailed Skimmers are found around lakes, ponds and, sometimes, slow-moving waters. They are one of the first dragonflies to colonise new reservoirs and gravel pits. They will also be present around well-established heathland pools. Where the edges of water bodies are shallow, and there is suitable substrate and plant debris, the larvae will prosper as the water warms through the summer. The edges of these water bodies are usually un-vegetated, even bare.

Distribution

Black-tailed Skimmers are found across Europe, including Turkey and parts of northern Africa; they reach as far north as the south of Sweden and Norway. Within the British Isles they are found in central Ireland and in some southern and central areas of Wales. In England it is a common species in the south-east, Cornwall and up through the Midlands. Few records come from Northumberland, Cumbria and, especially, Scotland.

In Suffolk the current distribution is similar to that of the previous Atlas. It is widespread in the north-east, south-east and the far north-west of the county, though seemingly more local elsewhere, this distribution may to some extent

Black-tailed Skimmer, immature male. 24th June 2006.

R. Fairhead

reflect surveyor bias. It was a species unknown in Suffolk until the last century. As stated by Mendel (1992) *"on 3rd June 1935 its presence was confirmed by a specimen observed in the Shipmeadow Marshes"*. It spread slowly until being well-established along the Waveney by the end of the 1940s. It probably also colonised from Essex. Its spread was then aided by *"the flooded workings of the expanding sand and gravel industry"*. Farm reservoirs have also aided the spread of this species and still do today.

As can be seen from the map, there are areas in the west where it appears to be absent, with some 10 km squares showing presence in only a single tetrad. It is possible that this species is under-recorded because of farm reservoir access issues.

Orthetrum cancellatum

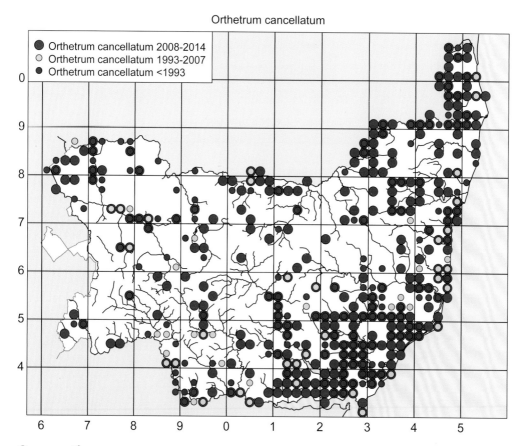

Conservation

The shading and silting up of farm ponds will not have helped the species in many areas, especially central Suffolk. To a large extent this has, however, been offset by the construction of many new farm reservoirs, which can be attractive to this species (and also the Common Blue Damselfly).

BLACK DARTER   *Sympetrum danae*

A. Easton

Black Darter, male. Corton, Suffolk, October 2013.

Introduction
The Black Darter is the only small dragonfly that is almost entirely black. The males, when mature are largely black, with yellow markings on the abdomen. There are yellow stripes and three yellow spots on the black patch on the side of the thorax. The legs are black and they have a waisted abdomen. The wings are without colour at the base and the pterostigma is black. Females and immatures are mostly yellow with a prominent black triangle on the top of the thorax. Females have a small yellow patch at the base of the wing.

Biology
Like all dragonflies, the Black Darter has a three-stage life cycle; it begins life as an egg that is deposited in water by an adult female in late summer while she is in flight, often in tandem with her male mate. The eggs, which can be over 200 in number, are laid in acid bog habitats, which are well vegetated with mosses and rushes. The eggs will persist, or overwinter, until the following spring before hatching. The nymph stage lasts from two to six months and emergence takes place mainly in July and August. The lifespan of the adults is quite short, probably only two or three weeks, allowing enough time to mature and mate.

Habitat

The Black Darter is predominantly found in upland and lowland bogs and heaths. Habitats include raised bogs and blanket valley and basin mires. Breeding occurs in acid, nutrient-poor bog pools, sphagnum-filled hollows, emergent rush and sedge pools and ditches. The species does not tolerate poor water quality or shade.

Distribution

Black Darter is a circumboreal species, occurring in North America and across much of central and northern Eurasia. In Europe, its range extends as far south as the Pyrenees and Alps. It is widespread in northern and western parts of both Britain and Ireland, but becomes rarer towards more south-eastern areas. In Britain, good populations do however exist in the New Forest and the Surrey heaths. Suitable habitat is scarce in East Anglia, and in Suffolk the Black Darter is a rarity.

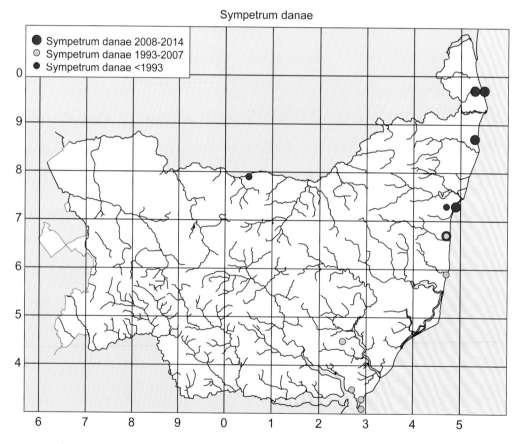

Sympetrum danae

A colony was first discovered by Morley in 1940 at Redgrave Fen, but this later died out; Mendel (1992) gives an historical account for this species. Currently, Black Darter does not breed in Suffolk, although it does in Norfolk at Grimston Warren and Roydon Common. It is, however, a recognised migrant. In 1995 there was a massive influx of dragonflies into the UK, dominated by Yellow-winged Darter *Sympetrum flaveolum* but including various other species, two of which – Scarlet Darter

Crocothemis erythraea and Banded Darter *Sympetrum pedemontanum* — had not previously been recorded in Britain. In Suffolk, as in some other counties, this influx included Black Darters, and individuals were noted on several dates at Felixstowe, Fagbury Cliff and Martlesham. Mendel and Marsh (1996) give a full account of this invasion of dragonflies in the Transactions of the Suffolk Naturalists' Society.

During the 2008–2014 Atlas period the Black Darter was recorded as a migrant at five coastal locations — all during the year 2013, when there was a significant immigration along the north Suffolk coast, peaking in early October. Although generally only singletons were observed at most sites, at least 24 were recorded at Corton on 7th October. Records there spanned the period from 26th September to 27th October; there was no expectation of breeding, however, since all individuals were males!

Conservation

As it does not breed in the county, there are no particular conservation concerns regarding Black Darter. Good quality pools or dykes in acid heathland could soon be utilised if it did colonise.

A. Easton

Black Darter, male. Corton, Suffolk, October 2013.

YELLOW-WINGED DARTER   *Sympetrum flaveolum*

R. Fairhead

Yellow-winged Darter, male. Gunton, Suffolk, 23rd July 2006.

Introduction

Yellow-winged Darter is characterised, as its name suggests, by having large yellow patches at the base of the wings. Otherwise it looks rather similar to many of the other red darters, though there are subtle differences particularly in the abdominal markings. The amount of yellow is typically so extensive – up to one third of the wing area – that confusion with species showing small amounts of yellow (e.g. Red-veined and teneral Ruddy Darters) is not normally a problem. It should be noted, however, that some Common Darters may show wings that are almost entirely amber-tinged. Yellow-winged Darter is only an erratic migrant to Suffolk and Britain, but may occasionally occur in numbers.

Biology

Yellow-winged Darter is a migratory species that may occasionally show large irruptions. Any breeding populations that become established in Britain are only short-lived, perhaps in part due to the species' dispersive tendencies.

Females oviposit either alone or in tandem, typically depositing eggs above the waterline onto damp mud, or even into completely dry depressions. The eggs over-winter, and following a rise in the water-table after winter rains, the larvae hatch out in spring. Subsequent development is rapid, with adults emerging later that summer.

The flight period lasts from June to October, adults being most common in August; records during the early part of the flight period, referring mostly to locally-bred individuals, are fairly rare in Britain.

Habitat

As with other darters, this species is associated with open marshy and grassy areas (hence the American term for the group as 'meadowhawks'). Breeding takes place in sunny, shallow, well-vegetated waters, or even in areas that are only seasonally wet. In East Anglia, the species has bred on occasion in fens and pingos. Migrant individuals may be found in a wider range of habitats, even well away from water – the most famous example being the large gathering noted at Great Yarmouth Cemetery, Norfolk, during the spectacular darter invasion year of 1995 (Heath, 1996).

Distribution

The species' range covers much of Europe, east to Japan. It is generally widespread and common in central and eastern Europe, but is much more patchily distributed further to the south and west. In these areas the exact range and status is often influenced by migration, influxes frequently establishing strong local populations which gradually dwindle over the years, only to be reinforced by further waves of immigration.

In Britain, migrants are most frequently encountered in southern and eastern counties, as might be anticipated for a migrant from the east, though there are also a sizeable number of records from south Wales and the Midlands (Cham *et al.*, 2014). In Suffolk, the species was first recorded at Tuddenham Fen in the west during August 1906 (Mendel, 1992). Occasional records continued in the county at irregular intervals thereafter, though none were reported during the intensive fieldwork for the 1980–1992 Atlas. During 1995, a mass invasion of Britain then produced a plethora of Suffolk sightings, mainly along the coast (Mendel & Marsh, 1996), and records at North Warren RSPB Reserve for some 4 years subsequently perhaps indicate the formation of a transient breeding colony, though this was never formally proven. There have been occasional further coastal sightings since then. In particular, small influxes were noted during 2006 and 2008. Over the last six years, no Yellow-winged Darters have however been reported from Suffolk, and indeed very few have been seen nationally.

Although the number of Yellow-winged Darter reported from the county has increased in recent years, this must largely be due to an increased interest in dragonflies, and hence to increased recorder effort. Influx years thus still remain rather erratic in timing. This contrasts with the situation for several other migrants seen in recent years, such as the Lesser Emperor and Red-veined Darter, which do genuinely seem to have increased in frequency. These species were thus either totally unknown or else extremely scarce in Britain, let alone Suffolk, until very recently. Many migrants to Britain are of largely southern origin, and have thus been greatly influenced by climate change over the last two or three decades, whereas Britain's Yellow-winged Darters appear to be primarily of eastern origin, and hence are subject to very different population pressures.

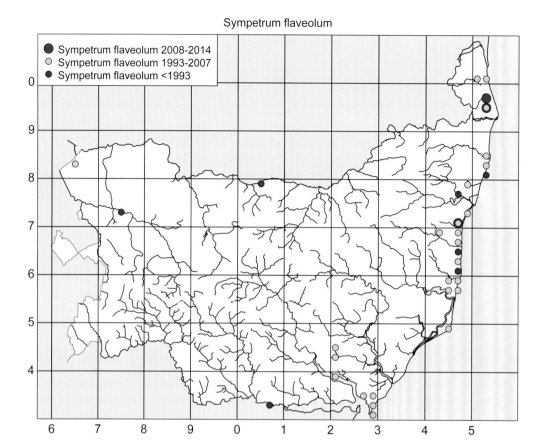

Sympetrum flaveolum

Conservation

As a migrant to Suffolk and Britain, no specific conservation issues exist. Breeding populations occasionally become established, but are short-lived. This appears to be an intrinsic part of the species' biology in western Europe, and permanent colonisation is perhaps unlikely in the near future.

RED-VEINED DARTER

Sympetrum fonscolombii

R. Fairhead

Red-veined Darter, male. Corton, Suffolk, 29th June 2006.

Introduction
In many ways a fairly typical darter, with the adult male being bright red and females and immature males being yellowish in colour. It is most conveniently separated from allied species by the blue basal section of the eye and by the pale pterostigma, strongly outlined in black. Females also possess characteristic abdominal markings.

Biology
The Red-veined Darter is primarily an immigrant to Britain, arriving in spring or early summer. Breeding may take place with any eggs laid developing rapidly. At latitudes equivalent to those of Suffolk, during good summers a second generation may then emerge in autumn (emerging individuals have been reported into November in Cornwall), though in poorer years and at more northerly latitudes, larvae may overwinter. Spring emergences the following year may then result, though none have so far been noted from Suffolk. It is believed that individuals emerging in autumn migrate back south before reaching sexual maturity; the fate of spring emergents is currently unclear.

Habitat
The species favours shallow, relatively sparsely-vegetated ponds and lakes for breeding – including gravel pits (an immature having been reported from Cavenham

Pits), balancing ponds, newly-excavated wader scrapes on nature reserves and the like. It also may occur on more typical lakes (it has, for example, been reported from Thorpeness Meare), and as a strong migrant may also on occasion be found well away from water.

Distribution

Red-veined Darter has an extensive world distribution, being found in Africa, south-west Asia and much of Europe. In Europe its strongholds are in the Mediterranean region, where it is a very common and characteristic species. Particularly as a migrant it may, however, also penetrate well to the north. Historically the species was only a rare and erratic visitor to Britain – there being only one confirmed Suffolk record, and one 'possible', mentioned by Mendel (1992) – but in recent years the species has become much more regular; a particularly dramatic influx took place in 2006. This shift in status is probably linked to climate change (Cham *et al.*, 2014), and the species has indeed been noted from areas as far north as Denmark, Sweden, Latvia and Finland over the last two decades (Boudot & Kalkman, 2015).

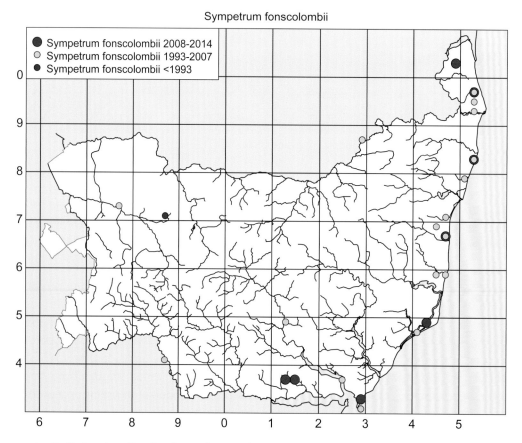

Sympetrum fonscolombii

- ● Sympetrum fonscolombii 2008-2014
- ○ Sympetrum fonscolombii 1993-2007
- ● Sympetrum fonscolombii <1993

In Suffolk, the distribution of records is quite strongly coastal, as is typical of a migrant species. During 2006, there was also a record from the far west of the county, when an immature female, quite possibly locally-bred, was noted at Cavenham Pits on 21st August. A male (not mapped) was additionally recorded from Lackford Lakes on 7th June 2015. There is one old record from Ampton Water (Mendel, 1992).

N. Mason

Red-veined Darter, male.

Conservation

Breeding has never been confirmed from the county, though an immature was seen at Cavenham Pits in late summer 2006 and oviposition was noted at both Corton Sewage Works and Gunton during the same year. Breeding attempts may also have taken place at Minsmere in 2002 (another good year for the species in Suffolk), when at least five adults were present there. The breeding status of Red-veined Darter in Britain is, however, complex. While some short-lived self-sustaining populations have been described from Britain, all locally-bred individuals that emerge in late summer/ autumn are believed to migrate south, rather than remain around to breed again locally. The extent to which the species could establish itself in the UK is thus uncertain. Whatever the exact situation, active conservation of the species is probably not a high priority since fresh immigration has the potential to 'rescue' populations that are declining.

RUDDY DARTER   *Sympetrum sanguineum*

M. Holland

Ruddy Darter, mating pair. Rendlesham, Suffolk, 30th August 2013.

Introduction

This species is smaller than the Common Darter. The males become blood-red with maturity, with a red frons and red-brown thorax. There is a very noticeable constriction of the abdomen around S4, giving a club-shaped appearance. An orange colouration can be seen only at the very base of the wings. The pterostigma is brown. There are usually two prominent black marks on abdominal segments S8 and S9. Females are duller and have an ochre/yellow abdomen and thorax. Older females may develop some red along the midline and segment boundaries of the abdomen. The all-black legs of the Ruddy Darter distinguish it from the otherwise very similar Common Darter (for other differences see under Common Darter).

Biology

Egg-laying takes place on the wing, with the pair usually in tandem performing a dipping flight low over the water. The female jettisons her fertilised eggs at the water surface or onto mud or detritus at the water's edge, areas where springtime immersion will prompt hatching. While the female is ovipositing the male may release the female and hover nearby to drive off any approaching males while she continues to lay the eggs. In common with the Common Darter, the Ruddy Darter exhibits the unusual ability to facultatively delay development of its eggs (diapause) or undergo immediate direct development.

The larval development period is one year; adult Ruddy Darters are on the wing from late June, rarely earlier (the earliest Suffolk record being 21st May [2011]), with a peak between July and the beginning of September. Late individuals may be seen into October, though there is some uncertainty over extreme dates as ageing male Common Darters can start to increasingly resemble Ruddy Darters, posing identification problems for the unwary.

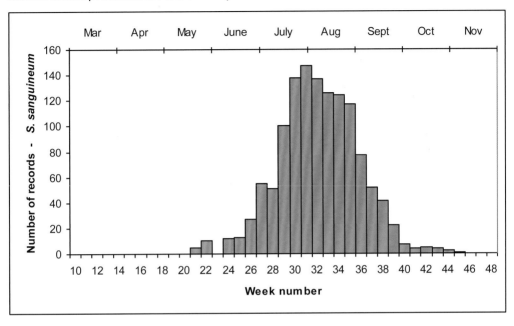

Habitat
This species inhabits quiet bodies of water that feature dense stands of semi-aquatic vegetation such as rushes and reeds. Other habitats include weedy ponds, ditches and occasionally sun-lit ponds in woodland. A common feature of preferred habitats is the likelihood that they will dry out in some seasons, leaving a growth of vegetation rather than bare mud. Gardner & MacNeill (1952b) suggests that the Ruddy Darter will only breed where the aquatic flora produces a tangle of strong roots amongst which the larvae can lurk. Generally, acidic and running waters are avoided, although this species may breed in slow-flowing sections of rivers where there is dense vegetation (Cham, 2004; Tyrrell et al., 2006). The temporary nature of many breeding sites also prevents the persistence of larval predators such as fish.

Distribution
The Ruddy Darter is a widespread species, occurring almost Europe-wide and ranging from North Africa to southern Scandinavia. The species is absent from the areas of the Alps north of Italy and the Mediterranean islands. To the east its range extends to eastern Siberia.

In Britain, it is found predominantly in the southern and eastern areas of the country. There has been considerable range expansion in lowland northern England (Cham et al., 2014). In Ireland, the species is widespread across the central plain and in some coastal counties but absent from all upland areas.

Sympetrum sanguineum

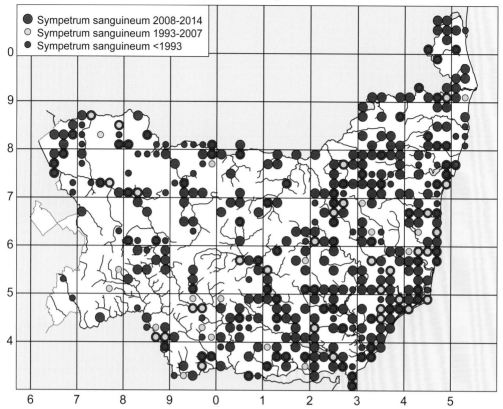

In Suffolk, Mendel (1992) summarises the historical status of this species but by the 1970s it was thought to be scarce and declining (Hammond, 1977). Mendel (1992) stated that *"Suffolk records support the view that its status, in the long-term, is determined by the level of immigration. Although there seemed to be a slow but noticeable increase during the 1980s, in 1991 the Ruddy Darter was suddenly rather common and widespread wherever there was suitable habitat"*. Without doubt, since the last Atlas (1980–1992), there has been a significant increase in numbers and distribution. The number of tetrads where this species is now being recorded has increased to more than twice that of the previous Atlas period. This species establishment may be due to climatic changes where immigration to bolster resident populations has increased and to the long runs of milder winters and drier summers, which may have benefited their preferred habitat requirements.

Conservation
The Ruddy Darter is categorised as of Least Concern in the British and Irish Red Lists. At a local level, habitat degradation and pollution still, however, have the potential to impact this species.

COMMON DARTER   *Sympetrum striolatum*

J. Kennerley

Common Darter, immature male. Woodbridge, Suffolk, 16th August 2009.

Introduction

The mature male is orange-red, though some can become darker red or more brownish with advancing age. Females and immature males are yellowish to light brown, the immature male starting to show pinky red patches on the abdomen as it develops towards the mature colouration; the legs are dark brown with a characteristic yellow stripe along their length. This species is most likely to be confused with the Ruddy Darter, but the male of that species has a 'waisted' abdomen and the legs are all black. It could also be confused with the rarer migrants such as Red-veined Darter and Yellow-winged Darter. However in the Red-veined Darter the underside of the eyes are blue-grey, while in Yellow-winged Darter the yellow patches at the bases of the wings are extensive and typically far more obvious than the small patches shown by other darters.

Biology

Ovipositing is done with the pair in tandem, the females dropping the eggs directly into water, usually over aquatic plants just below the surface. Lone females are occasionally seen laying eggs. Eggs typically hatch after 10 to 15 days and the adults emerge the following year. Both the Common Darter and the Ruddy Darter, however, exhibit the unusual ability to facultatively delay development of their eggs (diapause), presumably in response to specific environmental conditions (Corbet & Brooks, 2008). The flight period in Britain can extend from May until November, with occasional individuals even being seen in southern England during early December in favourable years. In Suffolk, the earliest emergence recorded was on 26th May [1982] and this species is usually the last species to be seen on the wing during the season, the latest record being 4th December [2008]. Burton (1948) provides an interesting account of egg laying, as acknowledged by Howard Mendel (1992).

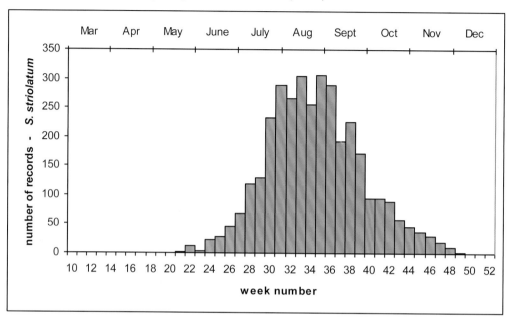

The species is a recognised migrant. Mendel (1992) quotes *"there are occasional records of huge swarms (Longfield, 1948), which are presumed immigrants into the British Isles from the continent and that there are some records from light vessels off the East Anglian coast (Dannreuther, 1937b)"*. There was a massive invasion of dragonflies into Britain during summer 1995, which was dominated by Yellow-winged Darter but included two species not previously recorded from Britain. Mendel & Marsh (1996) describe the Suffolk aspects of this influx; Yellow-winged Darter was prominent, with lesser numbers of Black Darter being seen. Their report also mentions immigration by Common Darter and Ruddy Darter. Evidence for occasional small-scale immigrations of Common Darter into Suffolk has continued through to the modern recording period, and indeed occasional recent records of individuals caught overnight in coastal UV moth traps, most notably by Matthew Deans at Bawdsey, may also refer to migrants. Parr (2006) discusses records of dragonflies from moth traps in more detail.

Common Darter, close up of mating pair. Aldeburgh, Suffolk, 16th August 2009.

M. Holland

Habitat

The Common Darter inhabits a wide range of habitats, but has a preference for still, shallow, often warm, stagnant waters and is a pioneer of newly created ponds. This species is able to colonise brackish waters and flowing streams and they make use of small water bodies and garden ponds of all sizes. They are frequently found away from water, resting on plants, bushes and bracken, or on sandy tracks in woodland rides.

Distribution

Common Darters are abundant throughout most of Europe but absent from northern Scandinavia, and the species' range extends to areas of North Africa and eastwards through Russia as far as China and Japan. The species is common and widely distributed throughout most of England, Wales, parts of Scotland and Ireland.

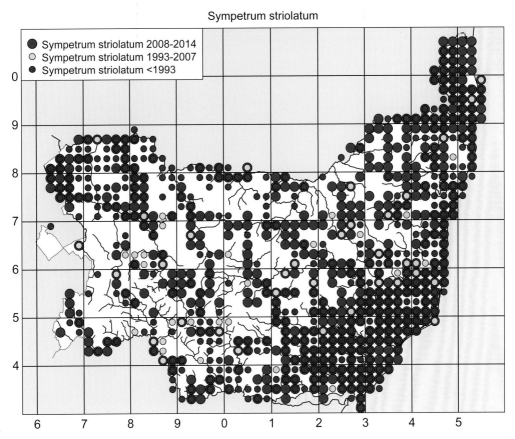

Sympetrum striolatum

In Suffolk this species appears to be as common as it has always been, and it is one of the most abundant. It is particularly numerous along the coastal strip and the estuary flood plains. Areas where distribution is patchy probably reflect a lack of suitable habitat, where waterbodies are either scarce or where water sources and tributaries have dried up in the summer months. Within this broad picture, some changes may, however, have occurred in this species' distribution. When comparing the latest Atlas results of 2008–2014 with older data, there appears to have been recent distribution gains, particularly in north-east and central Suffolk, unlike in north-west Suffolk where there initially appears to have been a decline in distribution. This apparent decline may, however, in part be an effect of reduced observer coverage. Visits to this region by Nick Mason and Adrian Parr towards the very end of the Atlas period have shown that Common Darter is in fact present in many, if not most, of the gaps they explored. It is true that when choosing areas to survey for dragonflies, the dry Breckland heaths will not be the first on many people's lists! Presumably many dragonflies in these areas are wanderers from further afield, and indeed numbers could vary from year to year.

Conservation

As this species is widespread, and immigration probably occurs from the Continent, there are no particular conservation concerns regarding Common Darter.

S. Aylward

Common Darter, male. Suffolk, 10th September 2015.

TRENDS IN THE SUFFOLK DRAGONFLY FAUNA

The results of fieldwork for the present Atlas show many similarities to, but also several differences from, the previous Suffolk Atlas, which covered the period 1980–92 (with most data being from focused recording during the period 1987–91). A number of factors need to be borne in mind when comparing the two data sets. Firstly, and most significantly, interest in dragonflies amongst wildlife enthusiasts has grown steadily in recent decades, and roughly three times as many records were received during the modern Atlas period as compared with the past survey. It is,

S. Plume

Scarce Chaser, male. Wheatfen Broad, Norfolk, 15th June 2013.

therefore, to be anticipated that many species might appear somewhat more common nowadays, simply as a result of increased recorder effort and coverage. Species such as the Common Darter, which has always been fairly common in Suffolk, illustrate the influence of recorder effects. It is worth pointing out at this point that despite an increase in overall recorder effort, parts of West Suffolk still remain relatively poorly recorded. This is due to a lack of recorders living locally, and to the degradation or loss of farm and village ponds over the last half century resulting in numerous areas that do not encourage casual visiting.

Whilst relatively minor changes in distribution or apparent abundance were noted for a number of species, several others showed more major changes that seem unlikely to be due simply to recorder effort. Species showing significantly increased distributions in the modern period compared to those found in the old Atlas include Red-eyed Damselfly, White-legged Damselfly, Norfolk Hawker, Hairy Dragonfly, Scarce Chaser and Four-spotted Chaser (Table 1). It has been suggested that some of the changes in abundance of Red-eyed Damselfly, White-legged Damselfly and Scarce Chaser seen along the River Stour may reflect, either directly (e.g. through introduction or transport of larvae) or indirectly (e.g. through habitat modification), the effects of a water pumping scheme that has seen water transfer from the Great Ouse in Norfolk/Cambridgeshire into the upper Stour at Kirtling Green and then ultimately on to reservoirs in Essex. Since it first started in 1972, the present day significance of this scheme is however unclear, although it may have been more relevant at the time of Mendel (1992). Certainly such a scheme cannot explain range changes seen for non-riverine species, or indeed for riverine species elsewhere in the county. Importantly, what is clear is that most of the species that have significantly increased their distribution in Suffolk over recent years are also spreading nationally (Cham et al., 2014). Some high level drivers are thus likely to be involved, and recent distributional changes may reflect both improvements in national water quality and the effects of changing climate. The onset of global climatic warming over the last 20–30 years is now well-documented, and is clearly having significant effects on British wildlife including dragonflies (Parr, 2010; Cham et al., 2014).

Since the Atlas of Mendel (1992), not only have a number of species greatly increased their Suffolk range, and some migrants from southern Europe such as Red-veined Darter have become more regular, several further species have appeared in the county for the very first time. These include not only the Scarce Emerald Damselfly, which has not had to spread too far from its Norfolk and Essex strongholds, but also species such as Willow Emerald Damselfly, Small Red-eyed Damselfly and Lesser Emperor, species that were essentially unknown from Britain, let alone Suffolk, only two decades ago. This surge in the appearance of new species for Britain is linked to ongoing range changes in continental Europe, and Suffolk, by virtue of its relative closeness to Belgium and The Netherlands, is well-placed to receive these newcomers. Indeed, despite a recent local spread, Suffolk still remains the national stronghold of Willow Emerald Damselfly, and the county also boasts the UK's only recent Large White-faced Darters. Although the precise origin of arriving

Table 1: Number of 10 km x 10 km squares (decads) from which species have been recorded.

	1980–92 Decads	2008–14 Decads	% change
Willow Emerald Damselfly	0	40	∞
Southern Emerald Damselfly	0	1	∞*
Scarce Emerald Damselfly	0	5	∞
Emerald Damselfly	47	45	-4
Banded Demoiselle	38	50	+32
White-legged Damselfly	3	6	+100
Small Red Damselfly	0	0	0
Azure Damselfly	51	56	+10
Variable Damselfly	10	11	+10**
Common Blue Damselfly	56	55	-2
Red-eyed Damselfly	17	50	+194
Small Red-eyed Damselfly	0	50	∞
Blue-tailed Damselfly	57	56	-2
Large Red Damselfly	41	57	+39
Southern Migrant Hawker	0	1	∞*
Southern Hawker	55	54	-2
Brown Hawker	50	54	+8
Common Hawker	0	0	0
Migrant Hawker	56	56	0
Norfolk Hawker	8	19	+137
Vagrant Emperor	0	1	∞*
Emperor Dragonfly	43	54	+26
Lesser Emperor	0	3	∞*
Hairy Dragonfly	14	44	+214
Downy Emerald	0	0	0
Large White-faced Darter	0	2	∞*
Broad-bodied Chaser	23	45	+96
Scarce Chaser	4	16	+300
Four-spotted Chaser	26	54	+108
Black-tailed Skimmer	49	53	+8
Black Darter	0	4	∞*
Yellow-winged Darter	0	2	∞*
Red-veined Darter	0	6	∞*
Ruddy Darter	49	52	+6
Common Darter	57	57	0

* Migrant individuals only ** Includes likely wanderers/transient populations

migrants or new colonists is rarely known for certain, Suffolk's Willow Emerald Damselflies may be an exception. After finding the first Willow Emerald Damselfly in Suffolk on 17th August 2007, Will Brame did some research and found that the timing coincided with the appearance in Suffolk of Bluetongue, a disease then new to the UK that effects ruminants and is spread by midges such as *Culicoides imicola*. Work done by Gloster *et al.* (2008) has shown that infected midges had most probably been carried across from the Ostend area of Belgium on a plume of hot air, and it is likely that the damselfly, or damselflies, arrived in Suffolk via the same route and at the same time.

In contrast to the positive fortunes of many species, especially those with fairly broad habitat requirements, there are just a few species that appear to be doing less well. Variable Damselfly suffered a significant decline, both nationally and apparently also in Suffolk, during the mid-twentieth century. While this now appears to have largely stabilised, with good populations still being found along the lower Waveney Valley and in the Minsmere area as well as at newly-discovered sites near Lakenheath perhaps resulting from habitat creation work there, some populations still extant at the time of Mendel (1992) have clearly since become extinct. Emerald Damselfly is another species that appears to have been lost from several sites in the county in recent years, although, on the plus side, some new ones have been found. On balance, an overall decline has, however, taken place, with records of the species accounting for only 1.6% of the total records received during the modern Atlas period, as opposed to 4.2% at the time of Mendel (1992) (Table 2). Although their overall distributions remain largely unchanged, both Blue-tailed Damselfly and Southern Hawker also show signs of recent declines, as reflected in the reduced frequency of sightings (Table 2). It is likely that habitat deterioration lies behind many of the negative trends found in the present Atlas, although it is pleasing to note that no species has been lost from the county list since the time of Mendel (1992). The newly-colonising Scarce Emerald Damselfly, however, still remains highly localised in Suffolk, so care must be taken to safeguard its future. Fortunately several of its sites are on Suffolk Wildlife Trust reserves, which should facilitate management.

In addition to changes in distribution, Cham *et al.* (2014) have shown that, at a national level, the phenology of some of Britain's dragonflies has started to change in recent decades. Most noticeably, several of the early-emerging species are now starting to emerge even earlier. This phenomenon is less obvious at a local Suffolk level, perhaps because of the smaller amount of data. Nevertheless, there are indications that ongoing climate change will have a significant effect on flight times in Suffolk. For instance, almost all record extreme 'First Dates' for the county's dragonflies have been set in only very recent years, whereas 'Last Dates' are more scattered, suggesting that recent increases in observer numbers/effort cannot alone account for this observation. The role of climate was particularly apparent during the springs of 2007 and 2011; that for 2007 was the third warmest on record in England, while that for 2011 was the warmest ever, with East Anglia showing a particularly high temperature anomaly (data from Met Office, UK). Many of the county's dragonflies were to see their earliest-ever recorded appearances during these two periods.

Table 2: Percentage contribution of each species to the total number of records received during various time periods.

	1985–92	2008–14	
	% of Total	% of Total	Change
Willow Emerald Damselfly	0.0	2.6	∞
Scarce Emerald Damselfly	0.0	0.1	∞
Emerald Damselfly	4.2	1.6	-61%
Banded Demoiselle	4.8	5.2	+8%
White-legged Damselfly	0.3	0.3	+14%
Azure Damselfly	6.8	8.9	+30%
Variable Damselfly	0.5	0.6	+13%
Common Blue Damselfly	12.4	8.0	-35%
Red-eyed Damselfly	0.8	3.4	+336%
Small Red-eyed Damselfly	0.0	1.6	∞
Blue-tailed Damselfly	18.6	9.5	-49%
Large Red Damselfly	5.1	5.9	+15%
Southern Hawker	8.4	5.2	-38%
Brown Hawker	5.7	5.8	+2%
Migrant Hawker	7.8	7.1	-9%
Norfolk Hawker	0.5	1.2	+136%
Emperor Dragonfly	1.9	4.9	+155%
Hairy Dragonfly	1.4	2.8	+101%
Broad-bodied Chaser	0.8	2.1	+167%
Scarce Chaser	0.4	0.9	+150%
Four-spotted Chaser	1.3	4.1	+215%
Black-tailed Skimmer	3.8	4.3	+15%
Ruddy Darter	3.3	4.0	+24%
Common Darter	11.2	9.7	-13%

Future prospects

Given that significant changes in the county's dragonfly fauna are underway, it seems appropriate to speculate on what further developments may take place. In view of the ongoing warming trends in the climate, further changes to phenology may be anticipated, as may be continued range expansions of warmth-loving species such as Small Red-eyed Damselfly and several of our current migrants and vagrants, which may indeed even go on to colonise; the Southern Migrant Hawker is perhaps one such candidate for colonisation. The appearance of yet further species new to Suffolk, or even the UK, is also perhaps to be anticipated. Species such as Small Emerald Damselfly *Lestes virens*, Goblet-marked Damselfly (or Blue-eye) *Erythromma lindenii* and Southern Darter *Sympetrum meridionale* are plausible candidates.

A. Parr

Goblet-marked Damselfly, pair in tandem. A possible future Suffolk species? Portugal, 4th July 2010.

While many of the effects of immediate climate change can perhaps be considered positive, this is not, however, universal. One of the most serious threats to Suffolk's dragonflies is coastal erosion and sea level rise leading to the brackish inundation of coastal freshwater grazing marshes. SWT's Hazlewood Marshes reserve, once noted for its rich dragonfly fauna is now an intertidal site, following irreparable damage to the sea wall during the tidal surge of December 2013. Although now a wonderful reserve for wintering and breeding wildfowl, Hazlewood Marshes no longer supports any dragonflies. Longer-term changes in sea level may in particular pose a threat to local populations of Norfolk Hawker, most of which are at very low elevation. Fortunately there are signs that, at least nationally, this species may now be expanding its range to include sites less prone to inundation.

Alongside climate-driven trends, changes driven by altered habitat quality are also to be expected. Outside nature reserves in Suffolk's farmed countryside, the loss of habitat through the abandonment of ponds and siltation of slow-flowing rivers continues to threaten dragonfly populations. But looking to the future, restoration of rivers driven by the European Water Framework Directive will continue to benefit many of Suffolk's watercourses. Projects to restore sections of the rivers Little Ouse, Black Bourn and Lark are underway and more projects to benefit other watercourses are planned for the future.

Agri-environment schemes provide the financial incentives for landowners to restore ditches and ponds and to create new wetland habitats. Unlike many invertebrates, dragonflies are powerful fliers and have good dispersal mechanisms so they can range over wide distances to colonise newly created or restored habitat. There is increasing evidence that if conservation is to be effective it needs to be planned at a landscape scale. Studies have shown that reduction in fragmentation through habitat connectivity is important to maintain populations and facilitate gene flow. If Suffolk Wildlife Trust's vision for a large-scale wetland in the Lower Waveney Valley (building on the existing nature reserves of Carlton and Castle Marshes) is realised, the perfect conditions will be provided to enable the populations of both common and scarce species to expand and colonise new areas.

Their acrobatic flying skills, fascinating behaviour and beautiful colours make dragonflies one of the most rewarding groups to record, observe and photograph. As current conservation efforts to maintain and extend suitable habitat come to fruition and the abundance and range of dragonfly populations increases, more and more people will get the opportunity to experience their beauty and wonder. Perhaps therein lies the future for Suffolk's dragonflies. With increasing public awareness, future efforts to conserve and extend their habitat and increase species' abundance are more likely to be successful.

A. Parr

Common Darter, male. Lackford Lakes, Suffolk, 21st September 2008. An attractive species, particularly in close-up.

REFERENCES

Askew, R.R., 1988. *The Dragonflies of Europe*. Harley Books, Colchester.

Beaumont, E. & Beaumont, A., 2012. Large White-faced Darter *Leucorrhinia pectoralis* (Charpentier) in Suffolk. *Atropos* 46: 11–13.

Boudot, J.-P. & Kalkman, V.J., 2015. *Atlas of the European dragonflies and damselflies*. KNNV Publishing.

Brochard, C. & van der Ploeg, E., 2014. *Fotogids Larven van Libellen*. KNNV Uitgeverij.

Brochard, C., Groenendijk, D., van der Ploeg, E. & Termaat, T., 2012. *Fotogids Larvenhuidjes van Libellen*. KNNV Uitgeverij.

Brooks, S.J. & Lewington, R., 2004. *Field Guide to the Dragonflies and Damselflies of Great Britain and Ireland*. 4th edition, British Wildlife Publishing, Hook.

Brooks, S.J., Cham, S. & Lewington, R., 2014. *Field Guide to the Dragonflies and Damselflies of Great Britain and Ireland*. Fully revised edition, British Wildlife Publishing, Oxford.

Burton, P.J., 1948. Suffolk Odonata of 1948. *Transactions of the Suffolk Naturalists' Society* 6: 238–239.

Cham, S., 2004. *Dragonflies of Bedfordshire*. Bedfordshire Natural History Society.

Cham, S., 2012. *Field guide to the larvae and exuviae of British Dragonflies: Damselflies (Zygoptera) and Dragonflies (Anisoptera)*. British Dragonfly Society.

Cham, S., Nelson, B., Parr, A., Prentice, S., Smallshire, D. & Taylor, P., 2014. *Atlas of Dragonflies in Britain and Ireland*. Field Studies Council.

Corbet, P. & Brooks, S., 2008. *Dragonflies* (New Naturalist Series, 106), Harper-Collins, London.

Daguet, C.A., French, G.C. & Taylor, P., 2008. The Odonata Red Data List for Great Britain. *Species Status* 11: 1–34. Joint Nature Conservation Committee, Peterborough.

Dannreuther, T., 1937. Migration records, 1937. *Entomologist* 70: 200–202.

Dijkstra, K-D.B. & Lewington, R., 2006. *Field guide to the Dragonflies of Britain and Europe*. British Wildlife Publishing, Gillingham.

Gardner, A.E. & MacNeill, N., 1950. The life-history of *Pyrrhosoma nymphula* (Sulzer) (Odonata). *Entomologist's Gazette* 1: 163–182.

Gardner, A.E. & MacNeill, N., 1952. Separation of *Sympetrum striolatum* (Charp) and *S. sanguineum* (Muller) (Odonata-Libellulidae). *Entomologists' Gazette* 3: 167–169.

Gloster, J., Burgin, L., Witham, C., Athanassiadou, M. & Mellor, P., 2008. Bluetongue in the United Kingdom and northern Europe in 2007 and key issues for 2008. *Veterinary Record* 162: 298–302.

Hammond, C.O., 1977. *The Dragonflies of Great Britain and Ireland*. Curwen.

Heath, P., 1996. The 1995 Yellow-winged Darter influx: a Norfolk perspective. *Atropos* 1: 12–17.

Jaeschke, A., Bittner, T., Reineking, B. & Beierkuhnlein, C., 2013. Can they keep up with climate change? Integrating specific dispersal abilities of protected Odonata in species distribution modelling. *Insect Conservation and Diversity* 6: 93–103.

Longfield, C., 1948. A vast immigration of dragonflies into the south coast of Co. Cork. *Irish Naturalists' Journal* 9: 133–141.

Lucas, W.J., 1900. *British Dragonflies*. Upcott Gill, London.

Maibach A., Vonwil G. & Wildermuth H., 1989. Nouvelles observations de *Hemianax ephippiger* (Burm.) (Odonata, Anisoptera) en Suisse avec évidence de développement. *Bulletin Société Vaudoise des Sciences Naturelles* 79: 339–346.

Mendel, H., 1992. *Suffolk Dragonflies*. Suffolk Naturalists Society.

Mendel, H. & Marsh, M.C., 1996. Invasion of dragonflies in 1995. *Transactions of the Suffolk Naturalists' Society* 32: 22–27.

Mitra, A., 2013. *Anax parthenope*. The IUCN Red List of Threatened Species; version 2014.3 Internet publication, http://www.iucnredlist.org/details/165488/0 [accessed 12 May 2015].

Moore, N.W., 1980. *Lestes dryas* Kirby – a declining species of dragonfly (Odonata) in need of conservation: note on its status and habitat in England and Ireland. *Biological Conservation* 17: 143–148.

Morley, C., 1911. Neuroptera (dragon-flies, stone-flies, lacewings, etc.). In: Page, W. (ed.), 1911. *The Victoria history of the counties of England. Suffolk.* Vol. 1. Constable, London.

Paget, C.J. & Paget, J., 1834. *Sketch of the natural history of Yarmouth and its neighbourhood*. Longman Rees and Simpkin and Marshall, London.

Parr, A.J., 2006. Odonata attracted to artificial light. *Atropos* 29: 38–42.

Parr, A.J., 2009. The Willow Emerald Damselfly *Lestes viridis* (Vander Linden) in East Anglia. *Atropos* 38: 32–35.

Parr, A.J., 2010. Monitoring of Odonata in Britain and possible insights into climate change. *Biorisk* 5: 127–139.

Parr, A.J., 2011. The year of the Vagrant Emperor *Anax ephippiger* (Burmeister). *Atropos* 44: 3–10.

Parr, A.J., 2013. The Large White-faced Darter *Leucorrhinia pectoralis* (Charp.) in Britain during 2012. *Journal of the British Dragonfly Society* 29: 40–45.

Parr, A.J., 2015. High numbers of Migrant Hawker *Aeshna mixta* (Latr., 1805) in Britain during 2014. *Atropos* 54: 29–37.

Parr, A.J., De Knijf, G. & Wasscher, M., 2004. Recent appearances of the Lesser Emperor *Anax parthenope* (Selys) in north-western Europe. *Journal of the British Dragonfly Society* 20: 5–16.

Phillips, J., 1997. Lesser Emperor Dragonfly *Anax parthenope* (Sélys) in Gloucestershire; the first British record. *Journal of the British Dragonfly Society* 13: 22–24.

Sherman, N., 2002. The discovery and observations of Small Red-eyed Damselfly (*Erythromma viridulum*) at a Suffolk site in 2001. *Transactions of the Suffolk Naturalists' Society* 38: 124–125.

Tunmore, M., 1999. Norfolk Hawker *Aeshna isosceles* record from the Breck district. *Atropos* 6: 33.

Tyrrell, M., Emary, C., Brayshaw, S., Sutcliffe, D. & Showers, J., 2006. *The Dragonflies of Northamptonshire*. Northants Dragonfly Group.

Glossary of some terms used in the Atlas

Abdomen – long hind section of insect behind the thorax; in Odonata comprising 10 segments (S1 – S10)

Acidic – having a low pH, less than 7.0

Alkaline – having a pH of more than 7.0

Anal appendages – claspers at the end of the male's abdomen used to hold the female

Andromorph – female that has male colouring

Anisoptera – the dragonflies (as opposed to damselflies)

Antehumeral stripes – pale stripes on the top of the thorax

Boulder clay – deposits of clay with glacial boulders and pebbles from glaciers or ice sheets

Brackish – water that is slightly salty

Costa – the leading vein on the front of the wing

Diapause – a state of suspended development, in either egg or larva, that occurs in response to environmental conditions

Emergence – when the larva leaves water and undergoes its final moult to become an adult

Emergent vegetation – plants that are rooted in water but grow above the surface

Eutrophic – rich in nutrients/minerals giving rise to abundant plant growth, often algae. Often leads to a lack of oxygen

Exuvia (plural **Exuviae**) – the skin/exoskeleton left behind when larvae moult; most typically applied to the final moult when the adult emerges

f. (as in e.g. f. violacea) – stands for form

Femur – leg segment above the knee

Fen – wet area, usually peat, fed by groundwater

Frons – top part of the front of the head (patterning sometimes diagnostic of species)

Immature – the adult after emerging until it is ready to mate. Colours may differ from that of the mature insect.

Iridescence – the property of some surfaces to change colour according to the light

Jizz – general impression of an animal and its behaviour

Larva – the part of the life cycle between egg and adult spent in the water

Lake – area of water larger than 2 hectares

Marginal vegetation – plants growing at the edge of ponds, lakes, rivers and streams

Marl – mud which contains lime and varying amounts of clay and silt

Neutral – having a pH around 7.0, neither acidic or alkaline

Ocelli (singular **Ocellus**) – simple light-sensitive organs found, in addition to the normal eyes, on the head of dragonflies and damselflies

Odonata – scientific term for the order that comprises damselflies and dragonflies

Oviposit – to lay eggs

Ovipositor – the female structure that is used to lay eggs

Pond – area of water smaller than 2 hectares

Pingo – Depression formed around the edges of glaciers or ice sheets during the Ice Age, frequently containing water

Pronotum – shield-like plate that covers the top of the prothorax (can be diagnostic of species)

Prothorax – small separate section at front of thorax where front legs are attached

Pruinescence – blue, waxy bloom that develops on some species (eg Emerald Damselfly, Scarce Chaser)

Pseudopterostigma – in demoiselle females it takes the place of pterostigma

Pterostigma (plural **pterostigmata**) – specialized cell towards tip of leading edge of wings; often darkened or patterned

River – flowing water more than 3 metres wide

S1, S2....S10 – numbering of abdominal segments (S1 being the most basal). The pattern on S2 varies amongst the different blue damselfly species

Semi-voltine – having a two year life cycle

Stream – flowing water less than 3 metres wide

Substrate – the material at the bottom of a water body, often plant debris

Swamp – wetland inundated with nutrient-rich water

Tandem – when male and female are joined together while mating

Teneral – newly emerged adult; exoskeleton non completely hardened and typically lacking full colour, wings shiny

Thoracic stripes – stripes on upper (dorsal) part of thorax

Thorax – middle section of insect. Where wings and legs are attached

Tibia – leg segment below the knee

Vice-county (or **Watsonian vice-county**) – geographical area used in biological recording; boundaries are fixed and not affected by any administrative changes to county boundaries

Zygoptera – the damselflies (as opposed to dragonflies)

Appendix. List of Key Sites for dragonflies in Suffolk

Site	Approx. Map Reference	Species of particular interest
Beccles Marshes	TM430920	Hairy Dragonfly; Scarce Chaser
Carlton Marshes	TM5092	Variable Damselfly; Norfolk Hawker
Campsea Ashe	TM330550	Hairy Dragonfly
Castle Marshes and North Cove	TM4891	Variable Damselfly; Hairy Dragonfly; Norfolk Hawker; Scarce Chaser
Corton Woods Pond	TM545964	
Culford School Lake	TL835705	Variable Damselfly
Darsham Marshes	TM420692	
Gipping Valley: Gt. Blakenham to Needham Market	TM120510– TM100540	Scarce Chaser
Gunton Pond	TM536958	
Haverhill Flood Park	TL655468	
Hopton Fen	TL990796	
Lackford Lakes	TL805705	Hairy Dragonfly
Lakenheath Fen	TL7086	Variable Damselfly; Hairy Dragonfly; Scarce Chaser
Lark river: Suffolk border up to Mildenhall	TL620820– TL710743	Hairy Dragonfly; Scarce Chaser
Leathes Ham	TM530933	Norfolk Hawker
Loudham Decoy Pond and Deben	TM315548	
Lound Lakes	TG511007	
Lowestoft Waste Water Treatment Centre	TM535979	
Market Weston Fen	TL983789	Scarce Emerald Damselfly
Minsmere	TM4666	Variable Damselfly; Hairy Dragonfly; Norfolk Hawker (+ migrant species)
Newbourne Springs	TM270435	
Oulton Marshes	TM505934	Hairy Dragonfly; Norfolk Hawker
Outney Common/Marshes	TM330900	Hairy Dragonfly; Norfolk Hawker; Scarce Chaser
Playford Mere	TM227463	
Redgrave Fen	TM050790	Scarce Emerald Damselfly
Scotland Fen	TM355475	Hairy Dragonfly
Shipmeadow	TM375910	Variable Damselfly; Hairy Dragonfly; Norfolk Hawker; Scarce Chaser

Appendix. List of Key Sites for dragonflies in Suffolk [cont.]

Site	Approx. Map Reference	Species of particular interest
Sizewell Marshes	TM470630	Hairy Dragonfly; Norfolk Hawker
Snape Marshes	TM395576	
Staverton Lake	TM360515	Hairy Dragonfly; high species diversity
Stour Valley: Nayland to Bures	TL970340– TL910335	White-legged Damselfly; Scarce Chaser
Stour Valley: Stratford St. Mary	TM040340	White-legged Damselfly; Scarce Chaser
Sudbury Common Lands	TL865415	
Sycamore Farm, Witnesham	TM200508	
Thelnetham Fen	TM017786	
Thorpeness Meare	TM470596	
Trimley Marshes	TM2636	
Ufford – River Deben	TM300520	
Walberswick NNR	TM4773	

ACKNOWLEDGEMENTS AND LIST OF RECORDERS

We thank the Suffolk Naturalists' Society and the Suffolk Wildlife Trust, who provided major support and encouragement. Clare Sheehan of the SWT helped with designing the front cover. Similarly, the role of Martin Sanford at the Suffolk Biodiversity Information Service, who helped with collation of records and preparation of the maps, is gratefully acknowledged. We are also most grateful for all the photographers who have allowed us to use their excellent photographs, even if they were not included.

In particular, we also thank the many people who submitted records to the Suffolk Naturalists' Society and to the British Dragonfly Society during the course of the present Atlas, and who thus made the publication possible. The following 'Principal Recorders' played a key role, by submitting in excess of 250 records each (figures in brackets indicate the number of records from each of the top recorders):

B. Buffery (849), R. Fairhead (911), J. Foster, S. Goddard (1161), P. Green, J. Hawkins, R. Macklin, N. Mason (2822), N. Odin, A.J. Parr (1580), M.F. Peers, M. Piotrowski (1500+), S. Piotrowski (2500+), J.P. Robinson, N. Sherman, A. Watchman, P. Wilkins.

In addition, records were received from:

S. Abbott, C. Adams, D. Adelson, D. Allen, R. Amor, B. Armour-Chelu, N. Armour-Chelu, P. Ashford, S. Ashford, R. Attenborrow, J. Austin, S. Babbs, C. Baines, N. Baldock, S. Baldock, S. Banks, P. Barker, J. Barnes, L.K. Barnett, I. Barthorpe, G. Batchelor, J. Baxter, A. Beales, E. Beaumont, G. Bennett, T. Benton, M. Berry, P. Bird, P. Bishop, D. Bradbury, W. Brame, M. Brewster, G. Brooks, J. Brooks, M. Broughton, D. Bryant, J. Brydson, T. Caroen, P. Carter, D. Casey, A. Chalkley, S. Cham, A. Chapman, G. Checkley, M. Christmas, P. Collins, P. Colman, J. Copsey-Adams, J. Coulter, T. Court, J. Cracknell, M.G. Creighton, H. Curry, J. Davis, J. Deacon, M. Deans, A. Dodgson, I. Downie, J. Dye, A. Easton, D. Eaton, R. Edwards, C.W. Emms, A. Excell, D. Fairhurst, J. Farooqi, M. Farrow, P. Feakes, D. Fincham, M. Forbes, R. Foster, B. Fountain, K. Fox, K. Freeman, S. Gant, R. Garrod, J. Gent, N. Gibbons, C. Gilbert, J.A. Glazebrook, A. Godfrey, I. Goodall, T. Goodfellow, D. Goodwin, J. Grant, M. Green, A. Gretton, G. Grieco, S. Grimwood, J. Halls, J. Hampshire, P. Hancocks, C. Hardy, D. Harris, J.P. Harrold, R. Harvey, C. Hawes, J. Haynes, A. Healey, D. Healey, B. Heather, B. Hedley, J. Hogg, B. Holland, M. Holland, P. Holmes, P. Hopkins, M. Hows, T. Howsham, C. Humphrey, J. Hunter, F. Ingall, C. Install, C. Ireland, C.A. Jacobs, M. James, J. Johnson, F. Jones, J. Kennerley, P. Kennerley, S. Kilshaw, K. Knights, D. Langois, P. Larcombe, R. Lee, E. Lemon, J. Levene, A. Livingstone, N. Lloyd, D. Longe, A. Looser, J. Lowen, H. Markwell, E. Marsh, M. Marsh, C. Mayes, C. McIntyre, D. McKenzie, D. McNeill, J. Middleton, J. Miller, C. Moore, D. Morley, M. Morley, K. Morris, J. Mumford-Smith, D.A. Murdoch, R. Murray, D. Newton, M. Nowers, P. Oldfield, J. Owen, L. Pankhurst, R. Parker, K. Parkes, R. Parks, R. Partridge, E. Patrick, H. Paxman, L. Peall, M. Pelling, V. Perrin, M. Pettitt, A. Piotrowski, G. Plank, C. Powell, M. Pratt, J. Pugh, P. Ransome, B. Raybould, S. Read, C. Reeve, K. Reeve, M. Reeve, M. Regnault, T. Reid, P. Rhodes, H. Rich, A.P. Richards, A. Riley, N. Roberts, C. Robson, N. Roche, K. Roe, J. Roughton, S. Routledge, R. Rozier, A. Sanders, M. Sanford, A. Saunders, P. Saunders, C. Shaw, G. Shaw, I. Shaw, R. Sheppard, N. Sills, S. Sills, M. Smith, P. Smith, A. Stanley, J. Stevenson, R. Stewart, R.G. Stewart, M. Stolworthy, S. Stone, W. Stone, D. Sutcliffe, B. Taylor, P. Taylor, H. Teagle, J. Thomas, A. Thompson, P. Thurston, K. Tubb, M. Tunmore, J. Underwood, P.J. Vincent, D. Walsh, A. Walters, J. Warnes, J. Webber, E. Wells, P. Wetton, L. Whitfield, C. Whiting, P. Whittaker, P. Wigens, A. Woodward, M. Wright, J. Zantboer.

Finally, a small number of records have also entered the system anonymously, and we thank the individuals involved with these.

INDEX OF SPECIES continued

INDEX OF SPECIES